AWAKE *to* Righteousness

Volume 2

A Study on the Book of Romans
Chapters 9 through 16

CONNIE WITTER

because of Jesus
publishing

Unless otherwise indicated, all Scripture quotations are taken from the Holy Bible, New Living Translation, copyright © 1996, 2004, 2007 by Tyndale House Foundation.
Used by permission of Tyndale House Publishers, Inc., Carol Stream, Illinois 60188. All rights reserved.

Scripture quotations marked AMP are from The Amplified Bible,
copyright © 1954, 1958, 1962, 1964, 1965, 1987 by the Lockman Foundation. All rights reserved.
Used by permission. (www.Lockman.org)

Scripture quotations marked NIV are taken from the Holy Bible, New International Version®.
Copyright © 1973, 1978, 1984 Biblica. Used by permission of Zondervan. All rights reserved.

Scripture quotations marked MSG are taken from The Message.
Copyright © 1993, 1994, 1995, 1996, 2000, 2001, 2002. Used by permission of NavPress Publishing Group.

Scripture quotations marked NASB are taken from the New American Standard Bible®.
Copyright © 1972, 1973, 1975, 1977, 1995 by The Lockman Foundation. Used by permission. All rights reserved.

Scripture quotations marked KJV are taken from the King James Version of the Bible.

Awake to Righteous, Volume 2, Chapters 9 through 16

ISBN: 978-0-9883801-6-5
Copyright © 2015 by Because of Jesus Publishing

BECAUSE OF JESUS PUBLISHING
P.O. Box 3064
Broken Arrow, OK 74013

Cover design and layout: Nan Bishop, Tulsa, Oklahoma
nbishopsdesigns.com
Edited by Rose Karlebach, Tulsa, Oklahoma
onlyroseofsharon@gmail.com

I dedicate this Bible study to my wonderful mom, Judy Beckham.

The very first person who told me the truth that I was "the righteousness of God in Christ Jesus" was you, Mom. Although I did not fully grasp its meaning at the time, a seed of truth was planted in my heart. This Bible Study is the fruit of you planting that truth in my heart and trusting Jesus to bring it out in my life.

Thank you so much for loving me and believing in me.

I love you and I am so blessed to call you Mom!

ACKNOWLEDGEMENTS

To those who faithfully attended the
Because of Jesus Ministries Bible Study
during the teaching of Awake to Righteousness. Your faithful
attendance and support contributed to the writing of this book.

I especially want to thank:

Nancy Bishop, Art Director

Rose Karlebach, Editor

Thank you for using your gifts to contribute to the publishing of this
Bible Study! You are both such a blessing to me!

CONTENTS

A Personal Note from the Author

Welcome to the continuation of our study on the Book of Romans! In Volume 2, we will finish our study of the Book of Romans that we began in Volume 1, as we read through chapters 9-16.

In the first eight chapters of the Book of Romans, the Apostle Paul taught us that righteousness is a free gift of God's grace. It is not something we earn by our good works or our obedience to the law. It can only be received through faith in Jesus! Now that we know that Jesus made us righteous, it means that we are innocent, blameless, forgiven, and qualified in our Father's eyes. As we awake to our true identity and realize that we are the righteousness of God in Christ Jesus, we find ourselves experiencing the joy and peace that comes from hearing the Good News of the Gospel. We realize that we are already approved, qualified and blessed because of the finished work of Jesus. We are the beloved children of our Daddy God, and the beloved bride of our Savior, Jesus, and nothing will ever separate us from their love! Romans 5:17 says that *those who receive [God's] overflowing grace and the free gift of righteousness … reign as kings in life through the one Man Jesus Christ. AMP* No longer living under the shame and guilt of our failures, we live in the freedom of our true identity in Him!

As we continue our study through chapters 9-16 of the Book of Romans, our hearts will continue to be established in the truth of the Gospel. The Apostle Paul teaches us about the great mercy our Heavenly Father has toward all of us. Christ is the end of the law as a means to righteousness for all of us who believe, and His gifts of holiness, forgiveness, and righteousness are irrevocable. He will never take them back once they are given. We can live in the security of His unconditional, unchanging love!

In Romans chapters 12-16, the Apostle Paul continues to teach us about our new righteous nature in Jesus. He instructs us in righteous living. He teaches us that our lives will be transformed as we allow the Spirit of Grace to renew our minds to the truth of our new identity! As we embrace the gift of righteousness, we'll find ourselves empowered to live a righteous and godly life. And it's not through any effort of our own, but by the power of God's Spirit. Instead of living under our own personal judgments of ourselves and others, we are free to live in the good opinion of our Father! We can now love, forgive, and accept others because we know we are loved, forgiven, and accepted by our gracious Heavenly Father.

As we finish our study of the Book of Romans, I pray you will awake to righteousness, and experience this life-transforming power of God's grace! As Romans 12:2 says, *"Don't copy the behavior … of this world, but be transformed by the [continual] renewal of your mind, and then you will experience the good, acceptable, and perfect will of God for your life!"* (Author's Paraphrase) Awake to Righteousness, and enjoy the glorious, grace-filled life your Heavenly Father has always planned for you!

Connie Witter

1. To make the most of your group study experience, we suggest you purchase the *Awake to Righteousness Volume 2* DVDs and downloadable *Leader's Guide* from the Because of Jesus website at www.becauseofJesus.com. A complete Bible Study Package is also available on our website for groups of ten (10) or more participants.

2. If you have more than ten (10) participants in your group study, we suggest you have several discussion leaders, one for each group, with a maximum of ten (10) people per discussion group. Keep in mind that the smaller the discussion group, the more comfortable each person will be in participating, and in sharing from their heart. You can print off multiple copies of the *Leader's Guide* so that each group discussion leader has a copy.

3. Hand out the workbooks a week before the study begins so that each participant has an opportunity to get his or her lessons done before the first week's meeting. In this way, the DVDs will be a review of the lesson they have already done.

4. Pray before you put in the DVD. Ask the Lord to open your eyes to the truth, and acknowledge Him as your true teacher.

5. Each DVD lesson will take approximately 50 minutes to view. Encourage the participants to take notes while they are listening so they can share what the Lord has shown them during group discussion. You will learn so much from listening to one another and from hearing yourself say what the Lord has taught you. What you share not only encourages others, but helps solidify the truth in your own heart.

6. Once the DVD is finished, have the participants break up into discussion groups of ten (10) or less participants.

7. Begin group discussion by asking each person what the Holy Spirit specifically spoke to him or her through the DVD teaching that week.

8. Choose a few questions from each day's study to discuss in your group.

9. Ask for any prayer requests and end your study with a word of prayer.

10. At the end of each group discussion, encourage participants to spend time with the Lord and in His word over the next week, and remind them of which lesson they'll be studying the following week.

Works Righteousness vs Faith Righteousness

Romans 9:1-33

Day 1

You Are a Child of the Promise

Day 2

You Have a Merciful and Loving Father

Day 3

Trust and Rely Upon Jesus

You Are a Child of the Promise

Romans 9:1-8

Pray before you begin.
Ask the Holy Spirit to reveal Jesus to you in the Scriptures.

Today we will study Romans 9:1-8. In these verses, the Apostle Paul explains that it's not your physical ancestry that makes you a child of the promise. When you placed your faith in Jesus, you received the gift of righteousness and the privilege of living as a beloved child of God. You are a child of the promise because of Jesus!

Romans 9:1-8: *¹With Christ as my witness, I speak with utter truthfulness. My conscience and the Holy Spirit confirm it. ²My heart is filled with bitter sorrow and unending grief ³for my people, my Jewish brothers and sisters. I would be willing to be forever cursed—cut off from Christ!—if that would save them. ⁴They are the people of Israel, chosen to be God's adopted children. God revealed his glory to them. He made covenants with them and gave them His law. He gave them the privilege of worshiping Him and receiving His wonderful promises. ⁵Abraham, Isaac, and Jacob are their ancestors, and Christ himself was an Israelite as far as His human nature is concerned. And He is God, the one who rules over everything and is worthy of eternal praise! Amen. ⁶Well then, has God failed to fulfill his promise to Israel? No, for not all who are born into the nation of Israel are truly members of God's people! ⁷Being descendants of Abraham doesn't make them truly Abraham's children. For the Scriptures say, "Isaac is the son through whom your descendants will be counted," though Abraham had other children, too. ⁸This means that Abraham's physical descendants are not necessarily children of God. Only the children of the promise are considered to be Abraham's children.*

Why was the Apostle Paul grieved in his heart? (verses 1-3)

_____

What had God given the people of Israel? (verse 4)

_____

Did God fail to keep His promise to save them? Why? (verse 6)

_____

Who are the true children of Abraham? (verses 7-8)

_____

The Children of the Promise are Those
Who Receive the Gift of Righteousness by Faith

In this passage of Scripture, the Apostle Paul is sharing his great sadness over the fact that many of his Jewish brothers and sisters had not received God's promise of righteousness. He continues to explain that even though they had been given the promise of salvation through Jesus, many of them had not received it by faith. In verse 6 he then asks this question, "Does that mean that God failed to keep His promise to Israel?" His response was an emphatic, "No!" because a person doesn't become a child of Abraham simply based on their physical birth and ancestry. You receive God's promise of righteousness through faith in Jesus. Romans 9:8 says that it is the "children of the promise" who are the true children of Abraham.

In Genesis 12:3, God made this promise to Abraham: *"In you will all the families and kindreds of the earth be blessed,"* and in Galatians 3:6-9, we see exactly what God meant when He made this promise to Abraham and his descendants:

> *"⁶In the same way, "Abraham believed God, and God counted him as righteous because of his faith." ⁷The real children of Abraham, then, are those who put their faith in God. ⁸What's more, the Scriptures looked forward to this time when God would declare the Gentiles to be righteous because of their faith. God proclaimed this good news to Abraham long ago when he said, 'All nations will be blessed through you." ⁹So all who put their faith in Christ share the same blessing Abraham received because of his faith.*

What blessing did Abraham receive because of his faith? (Galatians 3:6)

_____

Who are the real children of Abraham? (Galatians 3:7)

_____

What did God mean when He promised Abraham that, "All nations will be blessed through you?" (Galatians 3:8-9)

_____

_____

In order to understand the significance of this promise that God made to Abraham and his children, let us recall what it means to be given the promise of righteousness:

Righteous means: Innocent; free from guilt or blame; justified" (Strong's 1342, 1343, 1344)

> *It is the judicial act of God, by which he pardons all the sins of those who believe in Christ, and accounts, accepts, and treats them as righteous in the eye of the law. In addition to the pardon of sin, justification declares that all the claims of the law are satisfied....The law is not relaxed or set aside, but is declared to be fulfilled in the strictest sense; and so <u>the person justified is declared to be entitled to all the advantages and rewards</u> <u>arising from perfect obedience to the law</u> (Romans 5:1-10). It proceeds on the crediting to the believer by God himself of the perfect righteousness ... of Jesus Christ (Romans 10:3-9). Justification is not the forgiveness of a man without righteousness, but a declaration that he possesses a righteousness which perfectly and forever satisfies the law, namely, Christ's righteousness (2 Corinthians 5:21; Romans 4:6-8). www.christiananswers.net/dictionary/justification.html:Bible Encyclopedia*

According to this definition of the word *righteous* if you are a child of the promise, then you are innocent, free from all guilt, and justified in the Father's sight. He has pardoned all your sins through faith in Jesus, and accounts, accepts, and treats you as righteous in the eye of the law. You are an heir to all the rewards; one who is declared righteous by God, Himself! Not only has He forgiven all your sins forever, but you've been given a righteousness that perfectly and forever satisfies the law! You've been given the gift of the perfect righteousness of Jesus. You are a child of the promise!

You Are not a Child of the Slave Woman, You Are a Child of the Free Woman!

Galatians 4:21-31: *²¹Tell me, you who want to live under the law, do you know what the law actually says? ²²The Scriptures say that Abraham had two sons, one from his slave wife and one from his freeborn wife. ²³The son of the slave wife was born in <u>a human attempt</u> to bring about the fulfillment of God's promise. But the son of the freeborn wife was born as <u>God's own fulfillment of His promise.</u> ²⁴These two women serve as an illustration of God's two covenants. The first woman, Hagar, represents Mount Sinai where <u>people received the law that enslaved them</u>. ²⁵ And now Jerusalem is just like Mount Sinai in Arabia, because she and her children <u>live in slavery to the law</u>. ²⁶ But the other woman, Sarah, represents the heavenly Jerusalem. <u>She is the free woman, and she is our mother.</u> ²⁷As Isaiah said, "Rejoice, O childless woman,* *you who have never given birth! Break into a joyful shout, you who have never been in labor! For the desolate woman now has more children than the woman who lives with her husband!"* ²⁸ *And you, dear brothers and sisters, are <u>children of the promise, just like Isaac.</u>* ²⁹ *But you are now being persecuted by those who want you to keep the law, just as Ishmael, <u>the child born by human effort</u>, persecuted Isaac, the child <u>born by the power of the Spirit.</u>* ³⁰ *But what do the Scriptures say about that? "Get rid of the slave and her son, for the son of the slave woman will not share the inheritance with the free woman's son."* ³¹ *So, dear brothers and sisters, we are not children of the slave woman; <u>we are children of the free woman.</u>*

How was the child of the slave wife born? (verse 23)

_____

How was the child of the free wife born? (verse 23)

_____

Verse 24 says that Hagar and Sarah represent two different covenants. Hagar represents the covenant based on the law, what did the law do to the people? (verse 24)

_____

_____

Sarah represents the covenant based on God's promise. If you placed your faith in Jesus, Sarah is your mother, so what does that make you? (verses 28 and 31)

_____

_____

Who will persecute the children of the promise? (verse 29)

_____

Hagar and Sarah represents two different covenants. Abraham's first-born son, Ishmael, was born from his slave wife, Hagar, and represents a human attempt to bring about the fulfillment of God's promise. It is based on man's effort to make himself righteous through his obedience to the law. Works righteousness requires that man earn the promise of righteousness, and ultimately creates fearful slaves.

In contrast, Abraham's younger son, Isaac, was born from his free wife, Sarah, and represents God's fulfillment of His promise of righteousness through Jesus. Sarah represents the New Covenant, which is based on Jesus' righteousness and creates children who are free from the slavery of the law.

In Galatians 4:29 the Apostle Paul warns us that when we embrace righteousness as a gift, we will be persecuted by those who are still trying to earn righteousness by their obedience to the law. I, personally, have experienced this many times since I began embracing God's love and grace and resting in the finished work of Jesus! Those who are still trying in their own effort to be good will always come against those who are relying upon Jesus and living by the Spirit. So don't be surprised when this happens to you! We can pray for those who are still caught up in the law and ask our Father to reveal the truth to them. He revealed it to us and He can reveal it to them too!

God declares you righteous as a free gift of grace. You are no longer a fearful slave to a law that determines whether you are good or bad, but rather a beloved child of God that is forever good in His sight and led by His Spirit. While Hagar represents works-righteousness: man's attempt to get God's promise by depending on himself, Sara represents faith-righteousness: man receiving God's promise by depending on Jesus! Just as Galatians 4:30 says, those who are living as a slave to the law will not enjoy the inheritance of those who are living as a son who is free! Jesus made you a son who is free! You are a child of the promise of righteousness through faith in Jesus!

> John 1:11-13: *[11]He came to that which was his own, but his own did not receive him. [12]Yet to all who did receive him, to those who believed in his name, he gave the right to become children of God— [13]children born not of natural descent, nor of human decision or a husband's will, but born of God. NIV*

What was the main truth the Holy Spirit taught you from today's study?

_____

_____

_____

_____

_____

_____

_____

_____

You Have a Merciful and Loving Father

Romans 9:9-26

Pray before you begin.
Ask the Holy Spirit to reveal Jesus to you in the Scriptures.

Today we will continue our study on Romans chapter 9. This chapter has brought much confusion to the body of Christ. By reading Romans 9:9-26 out of context, man has come up with all kinds of wrong doctrine about God. But when we invite the Holy Spirit to reveal Jesus in this passage of Scripture and lead us into all truth, we will see the beautiful story of the Gospel and realize just how merciful and kind our Heavenly Father is to us all!

> Romans 9:9-13: *9For God had promised, "I will return about this time next year, and Sarah will have a son." 10This son was our ancestor Isaac. When he married Rebekah, she gave birth to twins. 11But before they were born, before they had done anything good or bad, she received a message from God. This message shows that God chooses people according to his own purposes; 12He calls people, but not according to their good or bad works. She was told, "Your older son will serve your younger son." 13In the words of the Scriptures, "I loved Jacob, but I rejected Esau."*

Like Abraham, Isaac had two sons, Esau and Jacob, a set of twins. Just as Hagar and Sarah represented two different covenants, in these verses Jacob and Esau are used to show the two different covenants again.

Let's take a look at verse 12. There is actually no record in Scripture that Esau ever served his brother Jacob. However, Esau's descendants — the Edomites — did serve Jacob's descendants (Genesis 32:3; 1 Chronicles 18:13). The prophecy that is spoken of in verse 12 refers to the nations that came from these two men. When the scripture speaks of "Esau" it is referring to the nation of Edom, which represents man's kingdom — works-righteousness — which is man's attempt to make himself right. "Jacob" refers to the nation of Israel, which represents God's kingdom of faith-righteousness, which is God's gift of righteousness to man through Jesus.

Moving on to verse 13, many people have interpreted it literally and have erroneously concluded that God accepts some people and rejects others. But when we understand the true Good News about Jesus, we can be very sure that God is not talking about Jacob and Esau as individuals, but rather the covenant that each of them represents. We know that God does not accept some and reject others, because 1 Timothy 2:4 says God wishes *"all men to be saved and to come to the knowledge of the truth"* NASB.

With this in mind, verse 13 can clearly be understood to mean*: "I love 'faith-righteousness' (man depending on Jesus), but 'works-righteousness' (man depending upon himself) I have rejected!"* Our merciful loving Father makes His children righteous, not based on their good works, but simply by having mercy on them all. He calls unrighteous people, "righteous" as a gift of His love, through simple faith in Jesus!

> Romans 9:14-16: *14Are we saying, then, that God was unfair? Of course not! 15For God said to Moses, "I will show mercy to anyone I choose, and I will show compassion to anyone I choose." 16So it is God who decides to show mercy. We can neither choose it nor work for it.*
>
> *16So then [God's gift] is not a question of human will and human effort, but of God's mercy. [It depends not on one's own willingness nor on his strenuous exertion as in running a race, but on God's having mercy on him.]" AMP*

To whom does God show mercy to? (verse 15)

_____

Can we choose God's mercy or work to earn it? (verse 16)

_____

Verse 14 poses an interesting question: "Are we saying then, that God is unfair because He accepts faith righteousness, but He rejects works righteousness? Is God unfair because instead of making a person earn righteousness, He gives it to them as a free gift? Is God unfair because He doesn't make people pay for their sins; He gives them mercy and freedom from their guilt instead? In verse 15 God said, "I will have mercy and compassion on anyone I choose." Now as humans we tend to think, "Murderers don't deserve mercy," or "That good person deserves God's blessing." That's how we would judge. But God judges in a completely different way than we would. He is God and He has chosen to have mercy on everyone, no matter how good or bad they are. Our Heavenly Father is so good that His gift of righteousness does not depend on a person's human effort, but on God having mercy on them. As the Scripture says, it is God who decides to show mercy. We can neither choose it nor work for it.

Romans 9:17-21: *¹⁷ For the Scriptures say that God told Pharaoh, "I have appointed you for the very purpose of displaying my power in you and to spread my fame throughout the earth." ¹⁸ So you see, God chooses to show mercy to some, and he chooses to harden the hearts of others so they refuse to listen. ¹⁹ Well then, you might say, "Why does God blame people for not responding? Haven't they simply done what he makes them do?" ²⁰ No, don't say that. Who are you, a mere human being, to argue with God? Should the thing that was created say to the one who created it, "Why have you made me like this?" ²¹When a potter makes jars out of clay, doesn't he have a right to use the same lump of clay to make one jar for decoration and another to throw garbage into?*

For some people, the passage we just read may seem to contradict what we know to be true about God. We know that He loves everyone in the world and sent His Son so that all who believe in Him might have eternal life (John 3:16). We know that Jesus laid His life down for all mankind to prove the value of every human being. So why does it seem like these verses are saying that God chooses to have mercy on some, but not all? In order to avoid confusion, we need to make sure that we understand the context of the entire passage. Let's continue to read the rest of this passage so that we don't miss Paul's entire thought process, and the Good News being shared:

Romans 9:22-26: *²² In the same way, even though God has the right to show his anger and his power, he is very patient with those on whom His anger falls, who are destined for destruction. ²³He does this to make the riches of His glory shine even brighter on those to whom He shows mercy, who were prepared in advance for glory. ²⁴And we are among those whom he selected, both from the Jews and from the Gentiles. NLT*

²⁵Just as He says in Hosea, Those who were not My people <u>I will call My people</u>, and her who was not beloved [I will call] My beloved. ²⁶And it shall be that in the very place where it was said to them, You are not My people, they <u>shall be called sons of the living God</u>. AMP

In this passage of Scripture we see the true heart of God. Read verse 22 again. In this verse, we see that even though God has the right to punish people who act badly, does He do that? How does He act toward them?

_____

Why is He patient with them? (verse 23)

_____

Who has God chosen to have mercy on? (verse 24)

_____

What does He call you and me? (verses 25-26)

In Romans 9:17-18 God said that He had appointed Pharaoh for the purpose of displaying His saving power throughout the earth. To do so, He hardened Pharaoh's heart so that His plan could be fully accomplished. Now God could have softened Pharaoh's heart and given his people favor with Pharaoh, but if He had done so, Pharaoh would have taken credit for their deliverance. He obviously didn't want any man to get credit for the salvation of His people. And He also demonstrated that no man will stand in the way of Him fulfilling His promise. God was resolved to show His power over the river, the insects, the animals, the meteors, the air, and the sun, all of which were worshipped by the nation of Egypt, and other nations had learned from their idolatry. God had a greater purpose then just delivering the children of Israel. He also wanted the Egyptians, and their neighboring nations, to hear of all His wonders, and turn from their idolatry to worship the one true God. In Joshua 6:17-23, Rahab and her family are a perfect example of this. Her heart was turned from idolatry, to faith in God, when she saw God's delivering power for Israel, and as a result her whole family was saved!

In Romans 9:19-26 Paul explains God's beautiful plan of redemption for every man. God did not just love the Israelites, He loved the Gentiles too, and His plan of salvation included everyone. Under the New Covenant of Grace, when you receive His gift of righteousness by placing your faith in Jesus, He forms you into a brand new creation. He transforms you from a broken vessel that is marred by sin and shame, and forms you into a vessel of honor. He makes you His righteous son or daughter who is perfect, blameless and without fault in His sight. He stands back with love in His eyes, and whispers, *"How beautiful you are my beloved, there is no flaw in you! You are my masterpiece!"* [Song of Songs 4:7]

Ephesians 2:10: *For we are God's masterpiece. He has created us anew in Christ Jesus, so we can do the good things he planned for us long ago.*

You and I once felt separated from God because of our sin, but He has brought us near, through Jesus. Romans 9:25-26 says that He calls us His beloved! He calls us sons of God! We belong to Him and it delights His heart to make us His own! (Ephesians 2:11-19)

Our Heavenly Father is a merciful, good and loving Father and everything He does is for the purpose of drawing us to Himself. God is Love! His purpose in creating us was to love us and pour His grace and mercy on us all.

Romans 11:32 says, *"For God has consigned (penned up) all men to disobedience, only that He may have mercy on them all."* AMP

20

God has consigned all men to disobedience. In other words, there is no man — except Jesus — who has ever obeyed God perfectly. According to the law, every man deserves to be called a sinner, and no man can ever be declared righteous by trying to obey it. When we understand this truth then we can truly understand God's great mercy toward us. While the law demanded punishment, our loving Father gave us mercy and the gift of righteousness. Through Jesus, He proved His great love for us all!

What was the main truth the Holy Spirit taught you from today's study?

_____

_____

_____

_____

_____

_____

_____

Trust and Rely Upon Jesus

Romans 9:27-33

Pray before you begin.
Ask the Holy Spirit to reveal Jesus to you in the Scriptures

Today we will finish our study of Romans 9. In verses 27-33 the whole point of this chapter is made very clear. Our loving Heavenly Father wants us to give up works righteousness and embrace faith righteousness. He wants us to let go of trying to qualify ourselves for His blessing through our obedience to the law and receive the truth that Jesus has already qualified us! He has given us His righteousness as a gift of His grace!

> Romans 9:27-33: *²⁷And concerning Israel, Isaiah the prophet cried out, "Though the people of Israel are as numerous as the sand of the seashore, only a remnant will be saved. ²⁸For the LORD will carry out His sentence upon the earth quickly and with finality." ²⁹And Isaiah said the same thing in another place: "If the LORD of Heaven's Armies had not spared a few of our children, we would have been wiped out like Sodom, destroyed like Gomorrah." ³⁰<u>What does all this mean?</u> Even though the Gentiles were not trying to follow God's standards, they were made right with God. <u>And it was by faith that this took place.</u> ³¹But the people of Israel, who <u>tried so hard to get right with God by keeping the law, never succeeded.</u> ³²Why not? Because they were trying to get right with God by keeping the law instead of by trusting in him. They stumbled over the great rock in their path. ³³God warned them of this in the Scriptures when he said, "I am placing a stone in Jerusalem that makes people stumble, a rock that makes them fall. But anyone who trusts in him will never be disgraced." NLT*
>
> *³³...Behold I am laying in Zion a Stone that will make men stumble, a Rock that will make them fall; but he who believes in Him [who adheres to, trusts in, and relies on Him] shall not be put to shame nor be disappointed in his expectations. AMP*

How were the Gentiles made righteous in God's sight? (verse 30)

_____

What did the people of Israel try so hard to do? Did they succeed? Why not? (verses 31-32)

_____

_____

Who were they stumbling over? (verse 32)

_____

What does God promise to those who place their faith in Jesus? (verse 33)

_____

In Romans 9:30, Paul asks the question which is on everyone's mind: "What does all this mean?" In other words, "What is the point of this chapter?" The answer to this question is clearly shown in verses 30-33.

Verses 30-33 tell us that the Gentiles never tried to be made righteous through obeying God's law, they simply received God's gift of righteousness through faith in Jesus. The people of Israel, however, who tried so hard to be approved and made righteous through their obedience to the law, never succeeded. Why? Because they were trying to be righteous through depending on what they could do instead of trusting in what Jesus did for them. They stumbled over Jesus. He was the Rock in their path. Instead of sitting down to rest in His gift of love, they continued to struggle in their own strength. They were *trying* instead of *trusting*. People who will not let go of the law as a means to make them right in God's sight will remain in slavery to it. They struggle through life never finding true peace.

The people of Israel were zealous for the things of God, but their faith was in their human effort. They thought they could earn God's favor by their good deeds. On the other hand, the Gentiles had no holiness to trust in, so when they heard the Good News — that righteousness was a gift of grace to be received through trusting Jesus — they gladly accepted it.

This same problem exists today. Some people are still trying to earn God's blessing and favor through their obedience to the law, not realizing that they will never succeed at being righteous through their own good works. *Trusting in Jesus is the only way.* When we hear sermons about what we must do to earn God's blessing in our lives and we try to do it, we are stumbling over the same stumbling stone that the people of Israel did. We are depending on ourselves instead of Jesus.

Those who trust in their obedience to the law and their ability to be good enough will live in continual condemnation and disappointment. You are never truly qualified for God's blessings by trying to obey it. This is the result of trusting in something other than Jesus to make yourself right in God's sight. On the other hand, those who trust that Jesus has forgiven them of all their sins and receive their true righteous identity as a gift of His grace will live free from condemnation and disappointment.

Like the people of Israel, I used to try so hard to qualify myself for God's blessings. Nearly every sermon I heard made me think there was one more thing I needed to do to please God. Constantly depending on myself to obey God's law so I could be blessed led me to disappointment. I finally realized I was stumbling over Jesus. He had already qualified me by giving me the gift of righteousness. He was right there offering me peace and rest in His love all the time.

How do you know if you're stumbling over Jesus? Just ask yourself this question: What do I think I need to do in order for God to be pleased with me? What do I think I need to do in order for Him to bless me financially, answer my prayers or bless my children? If the answer to any of these questions is a list of things you must do, then you are stumbling over the Rock in your path. His name is Jesus and He wants to give you rest from your human effort. He wants you to quit trying to be righteous in His sight by depending on your obedience to the law, and truly begin to trust and rely upon Him. You don't have to qualify yourself because He has already qualified you. The fruit of righteousness will come out in your life when you daily trust and rely upon Jesus!

So Awake to Righteousness!

Let go of works — righteousness and embrace faith — righteousness. Let go of any list of things you think you have to do to qualify for God's blessing. Give up trying to be righteous by obeying the law and begin to trust Jesus as your Righteousness! You are a child of the promise of righteousness through faith in Jesus. Trust and rely upon Him and you will never be put to shame. You are holy, blameless, qualified, and blessed in the Father's sight because of Jesus! Rest in His great love for you.

What was the main truth the Holy Spirit taught you from today's study?

Christ is the End of the Law for Righteousness

Romans 10:1-13

Day 1

Christ is the End of the Law

Day 2

It is Finished!

Day 3

Jesus is Your Righteousness

Christ is the End of the Law

Romans 10:1-4

Pray before you begin.
Ask the Holy Spirit to reveal Jesus to you in the Scriptures.

This week we will look at Romans chapter 10:1-13. Let us start with verses 1-4 in the Amplified Bible. We will gain a clear understanding that Jesus is the end of the law for the means of being made righteous.

Romans 10:1-4: *¹Brethren, [with all] my heart's desire and goodwill for [Israel], I long and pray to God that they may be saved. ²I bear them witness that they have a [certain] zeal and enthusiasm for God, but it is not enlightened and according to [correct and vital] knowledge. ³For being ignorant of the righteousness that God ascribes [which makes one acceptable to Him in word, thought, and deed] and seeking to establish a righteousness of their own, <u>they did not obey or submit themselves to God's righteousness.</u> ⁴For Christ is the end of the Law... as the means of righteousness (right relationship to God) for everyone who trusts in and adheres to and relies on Him. AMP*

Romans 10:4: *For Christ is the <u>end</u> of the law for righteousness to everyone that believeth. KJV*

Why was Israel's zeal for God not according to correct knowledge? (verse 3)

_____

_____

What did Jesus put an end to? (verse 4)

_____

Romans 10:2-3 tells us that the people of Israel had a zeal and enthusiasm for God. They had a desire to serve God and be approved by God, and yet it wasn't according to correct knowledge. They were completely ignorant of the righteousness that God gives as a free gift, and so they went about trying to be righteous through their good works.

These verses describe many in the church today. They have zeal and enthusiasm to live for God, but they strive to be acceptable to Him based on their performance, because they lack the understanding that the true Gospel is all about Jesus. They are completely ignorant of the truth that righteousness is a gift of God's grace, and so they spend their whole lives striving to establish their own righteousness. They do not submit themselves to God's righteousness — by giving up their ability to save themselves — and thereby rest in the finished work of Jesus.

Paul made it very clear in this passage that it's not possible to trust in our own righteousness and in God's righteousness at the same time. If a person believes that they have to do anything to earn God's blessing or is trusting in their own good works for His approval, then they have not submitted to God's righteousness. A person is either trusting in themselves and their own obedience, or they are trusting in Jesus and His perfect obedience. It is the latter which makes you righteous, acceptable and blessed in God's sight. The truth is, that Christ is the end of the law for the means of being made righteous, for all who believe in the finished work of Jesus.

Now let's look at the definition of the word *righteous* one more time so we can fully understand what it means to submit to God's righteousness:

Righteous means to be "innocent; free from guilt or blame; justified" (Strong's 1342, 1343, 1344)

> *It is the judicial act of God, by which he pardons all the sins of those who believe in Christ, and accounts, accepts, and <u>treats them as righteous</u> in the eye of the law. In addition to the pardon of sin, justification declares that all the claims of the law are satisfied. The law is not relaxed or set aside, but is declared to be fulfilled in the strictest sense; and so <u>the person justified (or made righteous) is declared to be entitled to all the advantages and rewards arising from perfect obedience to the law</u> (Romans 5:1-10). It proceeds on the crediting to the believer by God himself of the perfect righteousness, of Jesus Christ (Romans 10:3-9). Justification is not the forgiveness of a man without righteousness, but a declaration that he possesses a righteousness which perfectly and forever satisfies the law, namely, Christ's righteousness (2 Corinthians 5:21; Romans 4:6-8).*
> *www.christiananswers.net/dictionary/justification.html:Bible Encyclopedia*

According to this definition, the righteousness that God ascribes declares you innocent, free from all guilt, and entitles you to all the advantages and rewards as if you perfectly obeyed the law. The righteousness that God ascribes not only pardons all your sins, but gives you the perfect righteousness of Jesus as a gift of His grace! It is not something you earn by your obedience to the law, but rather a gift you receive through faith in Jesus. Christ is the end of the Law for the means of being declared righteous to all those who trust and rely upon Jesus!

Romans 13:1-4 tells us that because the nation of Israel was ignorant of God's righteousness, they went about establishing their own righteousness and did not submit to God's righteousness. What does it mean, then, to submit to God's righteousness? Man's righteousness is a person relying on their own ability or their own good works as a means of trying to earn God's blessing upon their life. God's righteousness is man receiving God's blessing and promises as a gift of grace.

Let me share a personal example of this from my own life. God promises to direct the paths of the righteous. His word says He will cause our thoughts to be agreeable to His will, and our plans will be established and succeed (Proverbs 16:3 AMP). How many times do we as believers worry and fret over decisions that we are making with these kind of thoughts, "Am I making the right choice?" "Can I hear from God?" "I don't know what to do." "What if I make the wrong decision?" When we think thoughts like this we are relying upon our own righteousness — our own ability to get it right — and not submitting to the righteousness that God ascribes to us through Jesus!

> *Roll your works upon the Lord [commit and trust them wholly to Him; He will cause your thoughts to become agreeable to His will, and] so shall your plans be established and succeed.*
> *(Proverbs 16:3) AMP*

Not too long ago, my husband had to make a major decision in his business. So he came to me to ask advice on what he should do. My reply to him was, "Honey, you hear from God. God causes your thoughts to be agreeable to His will and your plans are established and succeed. You will make the right decision!" Do you know why I was able to say that with confidence? Because God has promised to cause my husband's thoughts to be agreeable to His will. I was simply repeating what I heard my Father say about my husband.

So when my husband told me what he had decided, I confidently replied, "Then that's the right decision!" In the past I have had thoughts like "I hope that's the right decision. What if he didn't hear from God? Maybe I need to help him?" Those kind of thoughts are depending on my righteousness, depending on my own ability to get God's promise to come to pass in our lives. But now I know it's not my husband's responsibility to make his thoughts agreeable to God's will. It's God's promise to cause my husband's thoughts to be agreeable to His. This causes me to be able to completely submit to God's righteousness and not mine nor my husband's.

So, how do we submit to God's righteousness in this particular area of our lives? "Father, thank You for making me righteous in Jesus. You said that You would direct me in the way I should go. You promise to cause my thoughts to be agreeable to Your will. I submit myself to Your power and ability working in my life. For Christ is the end of my ability, and the end of me depending on myself to get it right." I trust Your promises to me!" That's what it looks like to submit to the righteousness of God!

Just to clarify again, let's look at the two kinds of righteousness: man's righteousness and God's righteousness.

1. **Man's righteousness** — striving to make yourself "right"

2. **God's righteousness** — being made "right" as a gift through faith in Jesus

As you submit to the righteousness of God by giving up your ability to be approved by God, or trying to earn any of His blessings, you will experience the abundant life that Jesus came to give you. The abundant life is not found in man's righteousness; it's found in God's righteousness.

So, how do you know if you've submitted to the righteousness that God gives through Jesus?

Ask yourself these questions:

What do I have to do to be financially blessed?

_____

What do I have to do to be healed?

_____

What do I have to do to be acceptable and approved before God?

_____

What do I have to do to get my prayers answered?

_____

What do I have to do to hear from God and be in His will?

_____

If your answer to any of those questions is anything other than trusting and relying upon Jesus, then you have not submitted yourself to the righteousness of God. You are still trying to be righteous on your own. "Christ is the end of the law" means it is the end of having to do anything to be approved and blessed by God, for everyone who believes! Believes what? Believes that Jesus has made them righteous and qualified them for every promise of God! If you have realized through this lesson that you have been depending on yourself to make yourself right, take time right now to talk to Jesus and submit to His righteousness. Rest in the truth that you are righteous, approved, favored, and blessed because of Jesus!

What was the main truth the Holy Spirit taught you from today's study?

_____

_____

_____

_____

_____

_____

_____

_____

It is Finished!

Romans 10:4

Pray before you begin.
Ask the Holy Spirit to reveal Jesus to you in the Scriptures.

Today we will look at Romans 10:4 again. We will pay particular attention to the meaning of the word *end* so we can get a clearer understanding of the meaning of this verse.

> Romans 10:4: *For Christ is the <u>end</u> of the Law… as the means of righteousness (right relationship to God) for everyone who trusts in and adheres to and relies on Him. AMP*

> Romans 10:4: *For Christ is the end of the law for righteousness to everyone that believeth. KJV*

What does this verse tell us that Jesus brought an end to?

_____

This verse says, "Christ is the end of the law as the means of being declared righteous." To whom does this apply? This verse tells us that Christ is the end of the law <u>for everyone who believes</u>. Jesus is the end of the law for everyone who trusts and relies upon Him and receives the free gift of righteousness that He gives.

The Greek word *end* in Romans 10:4 is the same Greek word found in John 19:30 when Jesus declared on the cross, *"It is finished!"*

Both of these words come from the Greek word *teleo* (G5055 and G5056; G5055 comes from G5056 Strongs) and they mean: "to end; that is, complete, execute, conclude, discharge (a debt): - accomplish, make an end, expire, fill up, finish, go over, pay, perform."

Christ is the end of the law as the means to being made righteous in God's sight. When Jesus said, "It is finished!" He was referring to the end of the law for the means of righteousness. Man would no longer have to pay the penalty for his sin; and man would no longer have to qualify for God's blessing through his obedience to the law. Righteousness was now given to man as a gift of God's grace. Jesus put an end to us trying to be good on our own. He put an end to our strenuous effort to qualify ourselves for any of God's promises. He qualified us forever by making us righteous when we put our faith in Jesus.

People who do not understand or receive the righteousness that God ascribes will never experience true peace. They are trying so hard to be good. They are trying so hard to obey God's law and get everyone else to obey God's law, too. 1 Corinthians 15:56 says, "the strength of sin is the law." But those who submit to God's righteousness and receive it as a gift will experience the fruit of the Spirit in their life. Galatians 5:22-23 says that the fruit of the Spirit is love, joy, peace, goodness, kindness, thankfulness, gentleness, humility and self-control. Against such there is no law. Preaching the law, by telling people what they have to do or not do to be approved by God and to qualify for His promises, will never set anybody free from sin. It will only put them in bondage to more sin and condemnation. It's only when we finally give up our own righteousness, and submit to God's gift of His righteousness, that we will truly live righteous lives.

The Apostle Paul is a perfect example of someone who gave up his own righteousness and submitted himself to the righteousness of God. Let's see what that looks like:

> Philippians 3:4-9: *⁴...though I could have <u>confidence in my own effort</u> if anyone could. Indeed, if others have reason for confidence in their own efforts, I have even more! ⁵I was circumcised when I was eight days old. I am a pure-blooded citizen of Israel and a member of the tribe of Benjamin—a real Hebrew if there ever was one! I was a member of the Pharisees, who demand the strictest obedience to the Jewish law. ⁶I was so zealous that I harshly persecuted the church. And as for righteousness, I <u>obeyed the law</u> without fault. ⁷The very credentials these people are waving around as something special, I'm tearing up and throwing out with the trash — along with everything else I used to take credit for. ⁸Yes, all the things I once thought were so important are gone from my life. Compared to the high privilege of knowing Christ Jesus as my Master, firsthand, everything I once thought I had going for me is insignificant — dog dung. I've dumped it all in the trash so that I could embrace Christ ⁹and be embraced by him. I didn't want some petty, inferior brand of righteousness that comes from keeping a list of rules when I could get the robust kind that comes from trusting Christ — God's righteousness. MSG*

What was it that Paul said He was tearing up and throwing out with the trash? (verses 4-7)

_____

_____

At one point Paul thought that making himself right by obeying the law was very important.

How did his thoughts eventually change? (verse 8)

_____

_____

What two different kinds of righteousness does Paul describe in this verse and which one was he embracing now? (verse 9)

_____

_____

The Apostle Paul is showing us in these verses that you can't hold on to your own righteousness (your obedience to the law) and embrace Jesus' righteousness at the same time. You are either trusting in yourself and all that you have accomplished, or you are trusting in Jesus and what He has accomplished for you.

When the Apostle Paul submitted to Christ's righteousness, he tore up everything he took credit for. He shared that he was done depending on his good works and his own efforts so that he could truly embrace Jesus and His righteousness.

Just like the Apostle Paul, I don't want the kind of righteousness that comes by trying to obey a list of rules, when I can have the perfect righteousness of Jesus Christ! I don't want the kind of righteousness that comes by my human effort at trying to be good enough, when I can be made right by God's grace through Jesus. The Apostle Paul said, "I give up my human effort. I give up all my good works so that I can embrace Jesus and be embraced by Him." This is what it means to submit to the righteousness of God. You give up your ability to hear from God. You give up your ability to love people. You give up your strenuous effort to be good enough and embrace His work inside of you. You embrace the truth that you are one with Jesus. He has given you His very nature, His perfect righteousness. As He is so are you in this world (1 John 4:17). You are loving, good, holy, innocent, and perfect in God's sight because you have embraced Jesus and He has embraced you. When you give up your own righteousness and embrace Jesus' gift of righteousness, you find true peace and rest in this world!

Let's read what the Apostle Paul said about this in Galatians 2:19-21:

> [19] For when I tried to keep the law, it condemned me. So I died to the law—I stopped trying to meet all its requirements—so that I might live for God. [20] My old self has been crucified with Christ. It is no longer I who live, but Christ lives in me. So I live in this earthly body by trusting in the Son of God, who loved me and gave Himself for me. [21] I do not treat the grace of God as meaningless. For if keeping the law could make us right with God, then there was no need for Christ to die.

What happened when the Apostle Paul tried to keep the law? What does the law do to those who try to be made right by it? (verse 19)

_____

_____

What did Paul stop doing so he could live free from condemnation? (verse 19)

_____

What did Paul begin to declare about himself and how did he live? (verse 20)

_____

_____

What truth did Paul share in verse 21?

_____

_____

The Apostle Paul taught us in these verses that if obeying the law could make you right before God then there would have been no need for Jesus to die for you. If righteousness could be gained by obedience to the Law, Jesus died for nothing. When we hold on to our own righteousness, we are treating the grace of God as meaningless. In a sense we are saying, "What you did for me, Jesus, is not enough. I still need to qualify myself and make myself right before God by trying to be good enough in my own strength. In these verses, the Apostle Paul had come to the end of himself. He found the secret to true freedom in Christ. He said, "When I tried to keep the Law, it just condemned me, so I gave it up to embrace what Jesus did for me!" The Apostle Paul knew that Jesus was the end of the Law for making him righteous and when Jesus said, "It is finished," He meant it!

What was the main truth the Holy Spirit taught you from today's study?

_____

_____

_____

_____

_____

_____

Jesus is Your Righteousness

Romans 10:5-13

Pray before you begin.
Ask the Holy Spirit to reveal Jesus to you in the Scriptures.

Today we will study Romans 10:5-13 and discover that the true salvation of our souls comes when we embrace Jesus as our Righteousness.

Romans 10:5-13: *⁵For Moses writes that the man who [can] practice the righteousness (perfect conformity to God's will) which is based on the Law [with all its intricate demands] shall live by it. ⁶But the righteousness based on faith [imputed by God and bringing right relationship with Him] says, Do not say in your heart, Who will ascend into Heaven? that is, to bring Christ down; ⁷Or who will descend into the abyss? that is, to bring Christ up from the dead [as if we could be saved by our own efforts]. ⁸But what does it say? The Word (God's message in Christ) is near you, on your lips and in your heart; that is, the Word (the message, the basis and object) of faith which we preach, ⁹Because if you acknowledge and confess with your lips that Jesus is Lord and in your heart believe (adhere to, trust in, and rely on the truth) that God raised Him from the dead, you will be saved. ¹⁰For with the heart a person believes (adheres to, trusts in, and relies on Christ) and so is justified (declared righteous, acceptable to God), and with the mouth he confesses (declares openly and speaks out freely his faith) and confirms [his] salvation. ¹¹The Scripture says, No man who believes in Him [who adheres to, relies on, and trusts in Him] will [ever] be put to shame or be disappointed. ¹² [No one] for there is no distinction between Jew and Greek. The same Lord is Lord over all [of us] and He generously bestows His riches upon all who call upon Him [in faith]. ¹³For "Everyone who calls on the name of the LORD will be saved." AMP*

If you are going to hold on to trying to be righteous by the law, what must you do to be righteous? (verse 5)

How can you give up your own ability to make yourself righteous and receive Jesus' righteousness? (verses 9 and 10)

_____

_____

What is true of everyone who gives up their own ability to make themselves righteous and places their faith in Jesus? (verse 11)

_____

Who does God generously bestow His riches upon? (verse 12)

_____

Who will be saved? (verse 13)

_____

Romans 10:5 says that the man who tries to be righteous through obedience to the law must live by it. In other words, if you are going to try to be righteous by the law, then you've got to do everything perfectly. You cannot mess up even once. If you ever sin or mess up, you are disqualified. If you are going to live by the law, you've got to be perfect in every way. So why would anyone want to live by the law? Let's give it up for the righteousness that God gives through faith in Jesus.

Romans 10:6-7 teaches us that the righteousness that is based on faith, does not say, "Who will bring Christ down or who will raise Him from the dead," as though we could be saved by our own human effort. Jesus is seated at the right hand of God, and has paid for righteousness for every man who will accept it. He's already gone into the abyss and paid the penalty for your sin. When we embrace what He did for us, we no longer depend on ourselves and what we can do to make us right before God, instead we completely rely upon Him as our Righteousness, and confess Him as the Lord of our lives!

When you realize that you could never be righteous by your own effort, and you submit to God's righteousness, you receive His gift of love by trusting and relying upon Jesus. Romans 10:6-10 tells us that those who have been made righteous by faith say, Jesus, You are my righteousness! You are my Lord and You rose again to secure my righteousness!" When you believe in your heart and confess with your mouth that Jesus is your Lord and your righteousness, you will experience His salvation. No one who trusts and relies upon Jesus to make them righteous will ever be put to shame or disappointed.

Jesus became our Savior when we placed our faith in Him and accepted His gift of righteousness. Now whenever we find ourselves in trouble, we can find peace by remembering that He made us righteous and He will rescue us as many times as we need to be rescued. He is our ever present help in time of trouble, not because we have done everything right, but because He made us right as a gift of His grace!

Let's read Romans 10:8-13 one more time in the Message:

> ⁸*So what exactly was Moses saying? The word that saves is right here, as near as the tongue in your mouth, as close as the heart in your chest. It's the word of faith that welcomes God to go to work and set things right for us. This is the core of our preaching.* ⁹*Say the welcoming word to God — "Jesus is my Master" — embracing, body and soul, God's work of doing in us what he did in raising Jesus from the dead. That's it. You're not "doing" anything; you're simply calling out to God, trusting him to do it for you. That's salvation.* ¹⁰*With your whole being you embrace God setting things right, and then you say it, right out loud: "God has set everything right between him and me!"* ¹¹*Scripture reassures us, "No one who trusts God like this — heart and soul — will ever regret it."* ¹²*It's exactly the same no matter what a person's religious background may be: the same God for all of us, acting the same incredibly generous way to everyone who calls out for help.* ¹³*"Everyone who calls, 'Help, God!' gets help."* MSG*

Jesus wants to be your Savior every single day! He wants you to quit relying upon yourself and truly live every day relying upon Him. When we try in our own effort we often get frustrated and anxious, but we can simply rest in the truth that Jesus is our Righteousness and all we have to do is call out for His help and He is right there to rescue us every single time.

Let me share with you a personal example of calling out to Jesus when I was in need of help. One particular day, I needed to go to downtown Tulsa for a 9:00 a.m. meeting. The problem was, when I got there all the parking places required cash, and I had no cash in my wallet. I was running late for a very important meeting and I didn't have time to go to an ATM to get money. So, I circled around the block a few times hoping to find a free parking space.

After about ten minutes of driving around trying to come up with a plan to save myself, I thought, "Maybe I should just park and pay the parking ticket later." I began to feel frustration and anxiety in my heart. As I felt those negative emotions, I realized they were the symptoms of me trying to save myself by not submitting to God's righteousness. As I struggled to come up with a solution to my problem, Jesus was patiently waiting for me to call out for His help! Finally, I gave up and called out, "Jesus! You said You'd help me in my time of trouble and I need a parking space right now!" I continued to talk to Him and thank Him for helping me, and as I did, I saw a parking lot that had no sign above it about the cost to park, and pulled into it.

As I got out of my car, I looked around again for a place to put money and thought, "Wow, a parking lot in downtown Tulsa that doesn't require money to park? That's great!" What was nice was that I couldn't have been any closer to the place I needed to be. I didn't have to walk several blocks; I just walked right up the stairs and there I was, right at my destination.

After the meeting was over, I proceeded to drive out of that parking lot, when I noticed a lady sitting in the booth, with the gate down, blocking my exit. Looking at the woman, I asked, "Does it cost money to park in this parking lot?" she replied, "Yes, ma'am, it does. Did you get a ticket when you came in this parking lot?" "No, ma'am," I said, "I didn't see any gate or ticket when I came into this parking lot." She said, "Didn't you see the gate when it was down? No cars can get in this parking lot without pulling out a ticket to make the gate go up." And I said, "Ma'am, I'm so sorry, but there was no gate when I came into this parking lot. I didn't see a ticket, and I have no cash to pay for it." She looked at me bewildered and said, "Ma'am, you mean you don't have a ticket?" And I said, "No, I don't have a ticket." She looked at me incredulously and said, "Okay, don't worry about it, just go on." As I drove away, all I could say was, "Thank You, Jesus!"

Now, I don't know how I didn't see the woman in the booth or how she didn't see me when I drove into that parking lot. I don't know how I got into that parking lot without pulling a ticket out and making the gate go up. I'm still bewildered by the whole experience. All I know is that I called out to Jesus and He came to my rescue. When I called for help, He was there to help me! That was my little trouble for that day. When we are done trying in our own effort to fix our problems and simply submit to Jesus' righteousness by calling out to Him, He shows up. He is our Savior yesterday, today, and forever!

So Awake to Righteousness

Jesus, You are my righteousness! I acknowledge that You died to pay the penalty for my sins and you rose again to secure my righteousness. I give up any attempt to save or rescue myself. I will no longer try to qualify myself through obedience to the law; for You are the end of the law as the means of making me righteous. I completely submit myself to your gift of righteousness. I thank You that I will never be put to shame or disappointed when I put my complete trust in You! When I call on You for help, You will always be there to help me, just because You love me! Thank you, Jesus!

What was the main truth the Holy Spirit taught you from today's study?

_____

_____

_____

_____

_____

_____

Works vs Grace

Romans 10:13-21; 11:1-11

Day 1

Faith Comes by Hearing the Good News About Jesus

Day 2

Works vs Grace

Day 3

The Law Blinds Us, But Jesus Makes Us See

Faith Comes by Hearing the Good News About Jesus

Romans 10:13-17

Pray before you begin.
Ask the Holy Spirit to reveal Jesus to you in the Scriptures.

Today we will look at Romans 10:13-17, learn the true meaning of the word *faith*, and get a clearer understanding that faith comes by hearing the Good News about what Jesus has done for us!

Romans 10:13-17: *[13]For "Everyone who calls on the name of the LORD will be saved." [14]But how can they call on him to save them unless they believe in him? And how can they believe in him if they have never heard about him? And how can they hear about him unless someone tells them? [15]And how will anyone go and tell them without being sent? That is why the Scriptures say, "How beautiful are the feet of messengers who bring good news!" [16]But not everyone welcomes the Good News, for Isaiah the prophet said, "LORD, who has believed our message?" [17]So faith comes from hearing, that is, hearing the Good News about Christ.*

Why is it important for people to hear the Good News about Jesus? (verses 14-15)

_____

_____

Does everyone who hears the Good News receive it? (verse 16)

_____

How does faith come to a person's heart (verse 17)

_____

What does faith look like? How is a person saved? (verse 13)

_____

In this passage of Scripture the Apostle Paul explains how important it is that people hear the Good News. He shares that faith comes by hearing the Good News about Jesus! In verse 13 we see what faith looks like in a person's life. It says that all who call upon the name of Jesus will be saved! Romans 10:13 in the Message Bible says, *"Everyone who calls, 'Help, God!' gets help."*

The word *"faith"* in Romans 10:13 comes from the Greek word "pistis" (Strong's G4102) and it literally means "reliance upon Christ for salvation; constancy in such profession."

True faith is simply relying upon Jesus to rescue and save you in every situation. True faith is simply saying, "Jesus, You are my righteousness! Help me, Jesus!" It's letting go of your ability to save yourself by your own works and embracing Jesus' righteousness that is given to you as a gift of grace. Romans 10:13 tells us that everyone who calls upon Jesus as their righteousness shall be saved!

But just as the Scriptures say, how can anyone call upon Jesus as their righteousness unless someone shares this Good News with them? The Good News is that Righteousness is a free gift. You don't have to earn it by your good works. It is simply the best Christmas gift you have ever been given. Jesus paid for it with His very life and gave it to you free as His gift of love!

In many other translations, Romans 10:17 says, *"Faith comes by hearing the word of God,"* but we must remember that Jesus is the Word of God (John 1:1). If we just hear Scriptures read, but Jesus is not revealed in those Scriptures, then faith (reliance upon Jesus) is not the result.

I have been attending church all my life and I can remember hearing sermons like "How to get my prayers answered," "How to be financially blessed by God," "How to hear from God," and many sermons on "Living by faith," but even though Scriptures were read out of the Bible to support these messages, none of them produced real faith in me. The reason was because the focus was on what I needed to do to be blessed, instead of what Jesus had done for me! I began relying upon myself to be right, when true faith is relying upon Jesus as my righteousness!

In contrast, when the true Good News about Jesus began to be revealed to my heart, I began hearing the Good News about the gift of righteousness. I heard that I am a virtuous, righteous woman, not because of what I have done, but because of what Jesus did for me! I am loved, approved, accepted, qualified, forgiven, equipped, and complete in Him! And the result of my heart hearing this Good News was true faith, which is relying

> True faith is simply relying upon Jesus to rescue and save you in every situation. True faith is simply saying, "Jesus, You are my righteousness! Help me, Jesus!" It's letting go of your ability to save yourself by your own works and embracing Jesus' righteousness.

upon Jesus instead of myself! The focus changed from me to Jesus and I began to truly believe that I can do all things through Him who strengthens me! I am sufficient in His sufficiency! Faith came to my heart when I heard the Good News about Jesus!

The Law of Works Points to You, the Spirit of Grace Points You to Jesus

Second Corinthians 3:6 says that the law kills and condemns, but the Spirit gives life. The reason the law condemns is because it focuses on what man needs to do to be righteous and reveals all the ways we fall short. The reason the Spirit gives life is because He came to reveal Jesus to us in the Scriptures and convince our hearts that we've been made righteous in Him (John 16:7-14).

> Jesus died to pay the penalty for all your sins and He rose again to secure your righteousness forever! He paid your debt and freed you from all guilt! He proved how very much He loves you by making you righteous!

In John 5:39, Jesus Himself said to the religious leaders of His day, *"You search the Scriptures because you think they give you eternal life. But the Scriptures point to me!"*

Scriptures alone do not bring life. It is a revelation of Jesus and His finished work on the cross that brings true life! It is only when Jesus is revealed in the Scriptures that true faith – reliance upon Jesus – comes to a person's heart.

When you hear a message that pretends to be the Gospel (it tells you what you need to do to qualify for God's favor and blessing) it produces self effort and self-reliance, not faith! It points people to relying upon themselves instead of Jesus!

So what is this Good News about Jesus that will produce faith in our hearts?

Romans 4:24-25: *²⁴[Righteousness, standing acceptable to God] will be granted and credited to us also who believe in (trust in, adhere to, and rely on) God, Who raised Jesus our Lord from the dead, ²⁵Who was betrayed and put to death because of our misdeeds and was raised to secure our justification (our acquittal), [making our account balance and absolving us from all guilt before God]. AMP*

This is the true Good News about Jesus:

1. The free gift of Righteousness (being declared innocent; forgiven; accepted; qualified) is granted to everyone who trusts and relies upon Jesus!

2. Jesus died to pay the penalty for all your sins and He rose again to secure your righteousness forever! He paid your debt and freed you from all guilt! He proved how very much He loves you by making you righteous!

Now let's take a test! Will the True Gospel, please stand up!

There are two messages being taught in the church today. One points to man's ability, the other points to Jesus:

1. **Works-Righteousness:** This message focuses on man's good works. It says: "If you want to be blessed by God, you must obey the law. If you do your part, God will do His! All of God's promises have conditions. You must meet the condition if you want to enjoy the promise!"

2. **Faith-Righteousness:** This message focuses on Jesus' finished work. It says: "You are blessed by God because Jesus obeyed the whole law! Jesus did your part so you could be declared righteous and enjoy His life! All of God's promises are "Yes" and "Amen" in Him! Jesus met the conditions for you so you can enjoy every promised blessing simply by trusting and relying upon Him!"

Which message produces true faith in your heart?

_____

Which message is really Good News?

_____

Remember true faith comes to your heart when you hear the Good News about Jesus!

What was the main truth the Holy Spirit taught you from today's study?

_____
_____
_____
_____
_____
_____
_____
_____

Works vs Grace

Romans 10:18 – 11:6

Pray before you begin.
Ask the Holy Spirit to reveal Jesus to you in the Scriptures

Today we will study Romans 10:18 – Romans 11:6. We will look at the difference between works and grace. Everything we receive from God comes by grace through faith in Jesus. When we revert back to relying upon our good works to earn God's blessing, we have fallen from grace and find ourselves experiencing fear, condemnation, and disappointment. It is important to understand that you can never earn what God has freely given! You cannot mix works with grace. You either receive from God by your good works or by His grace, but not both! Today we will see this truth taught very clearly in Scripture.

Romans 10:18-21: *¹⁸But I ask, have the people of Israel actually heard the message? Yes, they have: "The message has gone throughout the earth, and the words to all the world." ¹⁹But I ask, did the people of Israel really understand? Yes, they did, for even in the time of Moses, God said, "I will rouse your jealousy through people who are not even a nation. I will provoke your anger through the foolish Gentiles." ²⁰And later Isaiah spoke boldly for God, saying, "I was found by people who were not looking for me. I showed myself to those who were not asking for me." ²¹But regarding Israel, God said, "All day long I opened my arms to them, but they were disobedient and rebellious."*

Romans 11:1-6: *¹I ask, then, has God rejected his own people, the nation of Israel? Of course not! I myself am an Israelite, a descendant of Abraham and a member of the tribe of Benjamin. ²No, God has not rejected his own people, whom He chose from the very beginning. Do you realize what the Scriptures say about this? Elijah the prophet complained to God about the people of Israel and said, ³"Lord, they have killed your prophets and torn down your altars. I am the only one left, and now they are trying to kill me, too." ⁴And do you remember God's reply? He said, "No, I have 7,000 others who have never bowed down to Baal!" NLT*

⁵So too at the present time there is a remnant (a small believing minority), selected (chosen) by grace (by God's unmerited favor and graciousness). ⁶But if it is by grace (His unmerited favor and graciousness), it is no longer conditioned on works or anything men have done. Otherwise, grace would no longer be grace [it would be meaningless]. AMP

Romans 11:6 *And since it is through God's kindness, then it is not by their good works. For in that case, God's grace would not be what it really is—free and undeserved. NLT*

Did the people of Israel hear the Good News about Jesus? How did they respond? (verses 18-21)

_____

_____

Did God reject His people when they rejected Him? What was His heart toward them? (verses 1-2)

_____

_____

Did all the people of Israel reject the Good News? How did God encourage Elijah when he felt like he was the only one who had not submitted to Baal? (verses 2-4)

_____

_____

Did God choose to bless us and make us His own based on our good works or by His grace?

_____

If it is by His grace, then what can it not be based on? (verse 6)

_____

What is grace? (verse 6)

_____

It blesses my heart so much when I see in Scripture the loving heart of God even toward those who reject Him. Religion has often taught that God rejects those who reject Him, but we can see clearly in Romans 10:20-21 and Romans 11:1-2 that our loving Father has chosen us all! He opens His loving arms to those who turn from Him, and never stops inviting us to live in His love!

In Romans 11:3-4, the Apostle Paul tells us how Elijah was discouraged and complained to God because of those who rejected God. He felt like he was the only one who had not bowed to Baal. Baal was a pagan god that people worshipped. They believed to appease their god they had to sacrifice their children and inflict injury upon themselves in order for Baal to send rain or bless them. They chose a life of condemnation and trusting in their own works instead of trusting in the Good News about Jesus!

Many years ago when I began to understand the true Good News about God's love and grace toward me through Jesus, I felt like Elijah did in these verses. It seemed like everyone around me had bowed to religion and was trying to gain God's approval and blessing by their good works. It seemed that most people rejected the truth that righteousness was a free gift of grace and continued to bow to "Baal," which is the religious system based on man's works.

I was teaching a ladies bible study group about the love and grace of the Father toward them. I shared with them that they didn't have to try to be righteous, because they were already virtuous women in Jesus! Their righteousness was not based on their good works, but rather it was a gift of God's grace. At the time, I hadn't heard anyone teaching the true Good News about the finished work of Jesus. All I heard is what man had to do in order to earn God's blessing in their lives. When some people heard what I was teaching, some of them came against me and accused me of false teaching. They said, "It can't be that easy! It can't be just about what Jesus did, we must 'do' something if we want God to bless us!"

I remember one time talking to the Father, and saying, "Father, am I the only one pointing people to Jesus as their righteousness? Is there anyone else out there who has not bowed to trusting in their own good works and self-righteousness?" When I asked that question, the Holy Spirit brought me to Romans 11:4 and spoke to my heart through this Scripture saying, "No, Connie. You are not the only one. There are other people in this world that I am revealing the truth of my gift of righteousness to, and they are listening and their hearts and lives are being transformed just like yours!" What an encouragement that was to my heart! Since then I have seen many ministers rise up and declare the truth of God's love and grace through Jesus. They are not bowing to the religious system of man's performance, but rather embracing the finished work of Jesus! Many of God's people are letting go of their own self-righteousness and embracing Jesus' righteousness as their true identity! People are waking up to the truth that they are righteous because of Jesus, and it is transforming their lives. It is so wonderful to see so many people all over this nation and world sharing the true Gospel of Jesus Christ. It's just as the Scripture says in Romans 10:15, *"How beautiful are the feet of messengers who bring good news!"*

Now let's finish today's lesson by looking at Romans 11:5-6 one more time:

⁵So too at the present time there is a remnant (a small believing minority), selected (chosen) by grace (by God's unmerited favor and graciousness). ⁶But if it is by grace (His unmerited favor and graciousness), it is no longer conditioned on works or anything men have done. Otherwise, grace would no longer be grace [it would be meaningless]. AMP

Romans 11:6 in the New Living Translation says, *"And since it is through God's kindness, then it is not by their good works. For in that case, God's grace would not be what it really is—free and undeserved." NLT*

In these verses, the Apostle Paul confirms one more time that even though there are people who have bowed to "Baal" by trying to earn righteousness through their good works, there are those who have not bowed to the religious system based on man's performance, but have received God's grace for what it truly is — free and undeserved!

As verse 6 clearly states, it's only by God's grace that we receive every promised blessing of God! If is has to do with our good works, then grace is meaningless! If it is not a free gift, then its not grace!

Grace is the unmerited favor and blessing of God upon your life. Grace comes from the Greek word *charis* and it means "good will, loving-kindness, favour; the merciful kindness by which God, exerting his holy influence upon souls, turns them to Christ, keeps, strengthens, and increases them in Christian faith" (Strong's 5485, Blue Letter Bible)

Grace is not only the unmerited favor, loving-kindness, and blessing of God upon your life, but it is also His divine influence upon your heart that empowers you to trust and rely upon Him! Grace persuades your heart to believe that you are loved, approved, blessed, and favored because of Jesus!

You cannot mix works and grace. Just as Romans 11:6 says, you receive from God either by your works or by God's grace, but not both! There is no such thing as balancing works and grace. It is either all works or all grace! Otherwise grace is meaningless

Let's look at finances for an example. If you receive God's provision for your life because you gave, worked in the church, or was kind to someone, then His provision was not a free gift of grace, but rather something you earned by your good works. I remember when I was trying to earn God's blessing on my finances by the good works I did. For many years I heard messages about what I needed to do if I wanted God to bless me.

> Grace is not only the unmerited favor, loving-kindness, and blessing of God upon your life, but it is also His divine influence upon your heart that empowers you to trust and rely upon Him!

And so, I made sure I did what they told me so I could qualify myself. As far as this area of my life was concerned, I could say the same thing the Apostle Paul did, "I kept the law without fault." So when I didn't experience the financial provision that I thought I had earned, I became angry at God! That is what living by works does to your heart. If your motive for giving is so that you can be blessed, you judge others who aren't giving like you, and then like the older brother in the prodigal son story, you feel angry when it doesn't seem to be working for you!

But living by grace is so much different! When the Holy Spirit revealed to me that I can't earn any of God's blessings because they are all freely received as a gift of grace, my whole heart and life changed! I began to realize that I wasn't blessed by my Heavenly Father because of the things I did, but I was blessed because of what Jesus had done for me! This created thankfulness in me and brought back the joy of giving to my heart! When I looked to Jesus as my provision, His grace did a work in my heart and I experienced His abundant provision in my life! When you are relying upon your own ability and works, you think thoughts like this: "How am I going to take care of myself? What do I need to do?" "Am I doing enough?" But when you receive God's grace, you think thoughts like this, "Jesus, You love me. You are my Righteousness, and I know that You will provide all my needs. Thank You, Jesus, for leading and guiding me in the way I should go and opening doors of opportunity for me!" You simply receive His promises as a gift of His love to you, not something you earned by your good works.

This is what makes the Gospel such Good News: Righteousness is not a reward to be earned, but a gift of grace to be received through simple faith in Jesus. No one will ever be made righteous or qualified for God's blessing by their good works. It's only by grace through faith in Jesus that we will experience every blessing and promise of God upon our lives.

How Does a Person Fall from Grace?

Galatians 5:4-5: *⁴If you seek to be justified and declared righteous and to be given a right standing with God through the Law, you are brought to nothing and so separated (severed) from Christ. You have fallen away from grace (from God's gracious favor and unmerited blessing). ⁵For we, [not relying on the Law but] through the [Holy] Spirit's [help], by faith anticipate and wait for the blessing and good for which our righteousness and right standing with God causes us to hope. AMP*

How does a person fall away from grace? (verse 4)

_____

_____

How does a person live in grace? (verse 5)

_____

_____

   Many people have taught and believed that falling from grace was falling into
some kind of sin, but that's not what the Scriptures teach. Galatians 5:4-5 makes it
very clear that it is striving to be made righteous through obedience to the law that
causes a person to fall from grace. But when you live in grace, you no longer depend
on your obedience to the law to make you right. Instead you look to the Holy
Spirit for help and by relying upon Jesus, you anticipate all the good your Heavenly
Father brings into your life simply because He made you righteous as a free gift
of His grace! So give up any attempt to make yourself righteous by depending on
your good works, or a list of things you think you need to do and simply embrace
your true identity as a righteous, blessed, favored, loved, and approved child of God
because of Jesus! Live free in His grace!

What was the main truth the Holy Spirit taught you from today's study?

_____

_____

_____

_____

_____

_____

_____

_____

The Law Blinds Us, But Jesus Makes Us See

Romans 11:7-11

Pray before you begin.
Ask the Holy Spirit to reveal Jesus to you in the Scriptures.

In Romans chapters 10 and 11, the Apostle Paul talks a lot about the children of Israel rejecting God's gift of righteousness. The reason the children of Israel didn't embrace the gift of righteousness is because their eyes were blinded by the Law. As we have learned in a previous lesson, they believed they had to work to earn God's favor, and so they stumbled over Jesus! The law blinds people's eyes from the truth, but when a person turns to Jesus, their eyes are opened and they are set free!

Romans 11:7-11: *⁷So this is the situation: Most of the people of Israel have not found the favor of God they are looking for so earnestly. A few have—the ones God has chosen—but the hearts of the rest were hardened. ⁸As the Scriptures say, "God has put them into a deep sleep. To this day he has shut their eyes so they do not see, and closed their ears so they do not hear." ⁹Likewise, David said, "Let their bountiful table become a snare, a trap that makes them think all is well. Let their blessings cause them to stumble, and let them get what they deserve. ¹⁰Let their eyes go blind so they cannot see, and let their backs be bent forever." ¹¹Did God's people stumble and fall beyond recovery? Of course not! They were disobedient, so God made salvation available to the Gentiles. But He wanted His own people to become jealous and claim it for themselves.*

Why did most of the people of Israel not find the favor of God they were looking for? (verse 7)

_____

_____

What is God's heart toward those who continue to trust in their own good works instead of Jesus? (verse 11)

_____

These verses show why the children of Israel did not receive God's gift of righteousness. Verse 7 says their hearts were hardened and they could not see the truth. Self-righteousness hardens people's hearts. The Law was given so that people could see that the only way to truly be righteous is to give up their own ability to make themselves good and receive God's gift through Jesus.

Romans 11:8 can be a confusing Scripture. It seems to be saying that God shuts people's eyes and hardens their heart so that they can't see the truth. Anytime we read a Scripture that causes us to question the loving heart of the Father toward man, we can be very sure that we are not understanding the context of the Scripture. The heart of the Father toward those who have rejected His gift is made very clear in Romans 11:11. He never gives up on them! He gave His gift of righteousness to the Gentiles so that when the children of Israel saw the joy and peace that came as a result of His gift, they would want it and claim His gift of righteousness for themselves. It is His desire that all men might be saved and come to the knowledge of the truth (1 Timothy 2:4).

So why are some people's hearts hardened so that they cannot see the truth and how can they be delivered and set free from their slavery to the law? To get a clearer understanding of the answer to this question we will look at another similar passage of Scripture.

> Read 2 Corinthians 3:14-18: *[14]In fact, their minds were grown hard and calloused [they had become dull and had lost the power of understanding]; for until this present day, when the Old Testament (the old covenant) is being read, that same veil still lies [on their hearts], not being lifted [to reveal] that in Christ [the law] is made void and done away. [15] Yes, down to this [very] day whenever Moses is read, a veil lies upon their minds and hearts. [16] But whenever a person turns [in repentance] to the Lord, the veil is stripped off and taken away. [17]Now the Lord is the Spirit, and where the Spirit of the Lord is, there is liberty (emancipation from bondage, freedom). [18]And all of us, as with unveiled face, [because we] continued to behold [in the Word of God] as in a mirror the glory of the Lord, are constantly being transfigured into His very own image in ever increasing splendor and from one degree of glory to another; [for this comes] from the Lord [Who is] the Spirit. AMP*

The children of Israel's hearts were hardened. What did they lose the power to do? (verse 14)

_____

What does the veil on their eyes keep hidden from them? (verse 14)

_____

What happens when a person turns to Jesus? (verse 16)

_____

What do they experience when the veil is removed (verse 17)

_____

How is a person's life transformed when they begin to see Jesus clearly? (verse 18)

_____

When a person is trusting in their own righteousness, a veil remains on their eyes and they lose the power of understanding. They are not able to see the truth that in Christ the law is made void as a means of making one righteous. But there is freedom available to everyone! When a person humbly turns to the Lord, that veil is stripped away and all of a sudden the power of understanding comes as they behold Jesus! The Spirit of God begins to reveal Jesus and that person begins to experience freedom from the slavery of the law and liberty from bondage. As a person beholds Jesus as in a mirror, realizing that He gave them His very own righteousness as a gift, they are transformed from the inside out by the power of God's Spirit. No longer depending on their own human effort, now the Spirit of the Lord is at work bringing out the fruit of love, joy and peace in their life!

I have experienced this transformation in my own life. I used to read the Scriptures with a veil on my eyes. All I could see was the law of rules that I needed to do to be good and earn God's blessing! I had lost the power of understanding that the true Good News Gospel was all about Jesus. I was relying upon what I could do instead of what Jesus did for me! My heart was filled with condemnation, pride, fear, worry, and discouragement and I felt like nothing was going right in my life. When I came to the end of myself and was just about ready to give up, I turned to Jesus and simply said, "Jesus, show me the truth that will set me free!" When I did that, the veil was stripped from my eyes. All of a sudden I could see the beauty of Jesus and the gift of righteousness that He had so freely given to me! My heart was overwhelmed with His great love for me, and the Spirit of God set me free from my slavery to the law. The Word of God became life to me again as I beheld Jesus on every page. I was reading the very same Bible I had read hundreds of times since I was a little girl, but it was like a light bulb was turned on and I began to see Jesus in all His glory. I realized that "as He is so am I in this world." I began to experience 2 Corinthians 3:18, and as I beheld the glory of Jesus as though I was looking in a mirror, I was transformed from glory to glory by the power of the Spirit. I began to truly experience the fruit of the Spirit in my life!

The very first place the Holy Spirit took me to when the veil was lifted from my eyes was Proverbs 31. Previously, I had not liked this passage of Scripture because it only showed me how I did not measure up. When the veil was removed, I began to see so clearly that Jesus had made me a virtuous woman as a gift of His grace. I saw that I was already righteous and blessed because of Jesus. I saw that it is the Spirit of Grace that works this out in my life, not me. Producing the fruit of Proverbs 31 was not something that I had to do, it was a work of God's grace! Since I had this revelation, I have been transformed from glory to glory, and it did not come by depending on my own good works or human effort, but by the power of God's Spirit. The power of grace, "the divine influence upon my heart and its reflection in my life," was at work in me to manifest God's glory in my life!

> Galatians 5:22-23 says, *²²But the fruit of the [Holy] Spirit [the work which His presence within accomplishes] is love, joy . . . peace, patience . . . kindness, goodness . . . faithfulness, ²³gentleness (meekness, humility), self-control. . . . Against such things there is no law [that can bring a charge]. AMP*

Second Corinthians 3:18 says that as we behold Jesus as though we are looking at ourselves in a mirror, we are changed from glory to glory into His very image by the power of God's Spirit. According to Galatians 5:22-23 what work does the Spirit of Grace accomplish in us? What does God's glory manifested in our lives really look like?

_____

_____

_____

Galatians 5:22-23 reveals the very character and nature of God's Spirit. Our Heavenly Father is love! He is joy, peace, patience, kindness, and goodness! He is faithful, gentle and self-controlled. This is who God is and the fruit of His righteousness. We have been made righteous in Jesus and the Father has given us His very nature as a gift of His grace. It is His Spirit that brings this fruit out in our lives as we behold Jesus and trust what He has done for us and who we are in Him!

So Awake to Righteousness

You no longer have to live depending on your own ability or good works to be approved and blessed by God! Let go of your works and embrace God's grace! Look to Jesus, for He is grace personified! As you look to Him, and behold that you have been made righteousness in Him, the Holy Spirit will work in you and bring out the fruit of His Spirit in your life. No more work; there is only rest in the finished work of Jesus!

What was the main truth the Holy Spirit taught you from today's study?

_____

_____

_____

_____

Jesus Alone Qualifies You

Romans 11:12-36

Day 1

Jesus Made You Holy

Day 2

The Gifts of God Are Received by Faith

Day 3

God's Gifts Are Irrevocable

Jesus Made You Holy

Romans 11:12-16

Pray before you begin.
Ask the Holy Spirit to reveal Jesus to you in the Scriptures

This week we will finish reading Romans chapter 11. It is important to remember what we have learned so far so that we can understand fully what is being taught. Romans 11:11 said that the children of Israel had stumbled, but there was still hope for them to receive salvation. They had stumbled over Jesus by attempting to make themselves righteous by their own good works, instead of simply receiving the righteousness that Jesus purchased for them as a gift. (Romans 9:30-33). It is Jesus alone who qualifies us for all of God's blessings! Every promise we receive is a gift of His grace that is received by faith — relying upon Jesus! Today we will read Romans 11:12-16 and get a deeper understanding of the truth that Jesus made us Holy as a gift of His grace!

> Romans 11:12-16: *¹²Now if the Gentiles were enriched because the people of Israel turned down God's offer of salvation, think how much greater a blessing the world will share when they finally accept it. ¹³I am saying all this especially for you Gentiles. God has appointed me as the apostle to the Gentiles. I stress this, ¹⁴for I want somehow to make the people of Israel jealous of what you Gentiles have, so I might save some of them. ¹⁵For since their rejection meant that God offered salvation to the rest of the world, their acceptance will be even more wonderful. It will be life for those who were dead! ¹⁶And since Abraham and the other patriarchs were holy, their descendants will also be holy—just as the entire batch of dough is holy because the portion given as an offering is holy. For if the roots of the tree are holy, the branches will be, too.*

What was the Apostle Paul hoping would happen in the hearts of the people of Israel as a result of the Gentiles receiving the gift of righteousness? (verses 12-15)

_____

_____

God promised Abraham that he and his descendants would be blessed! You learned in week 1 that those who put their faith in Jesus are the true children of Abraham. According to verse 16, what is true of Abraham and His children?

You Are Holy Through Faith in Jesus!

The word *holy* in Romans 11:16 comes from the Greek work "*hagios* (Strong's G40). According to Vines Expository Dictionary, holy means: "<u>separated from sin and therefore consecrated to God, sacred</u>."

> "*It is evident that hagios and its kindred words, . . .express something more and higher than hieros, [which means] "sacred, outwardly associated with God"; something more than semnos, [which means] "<u>worthy, honorable</u>"; something more than hagnos, [which means] "<u>pure, free from defilement</u>." Hagios is... more comprehensive... It is characteristically godlikeness*" (G.B. Stevens, in Hastings' Bible Dictionary) BLB [bracketed text inserted for clarification]

Your Heavenly Father made you holy through Jesus. What does that mean? According to the Vine's Dictionary definition of the word *holy*, that means He separated you from sin and brought you to Himself. Sin is no longer part of who you are! You are holy and pure just like your Heavenly Father! He made you worthy and honorable. He made you just like Himself — godlike. This is not something you attain by your actions, but rather a gift of His love and grace to you!

> Ephesians 1:4 says, "*Even before He made the world, God loved us and chose us in Christ to be holy and without fault in His eyes.*"

When your Heavenly Father looks at you in Christ, what does He see? What did He do for you because of His great love for you?

There have been times in my life when I was dealing with difficult circumstances that I thought, "Something is wrong with me!" The enemy of my soul was tempting me to believe a lie about myself. If I believed this lie then my mind would go immediately to how I needed to fix myself and fix my own problem. This only produced condemnation in my heart and I became discouraged and hopeless in my situation. But when I called out to Jesus to help me during those difficult times, He reminded me that I am loved! I am chosen to be holy and without fault in my Father's eyes. In order for peace to reign in my heart, I had to take my eyes off the things I saw that were wrong with me, look to Jesus and embrace the truth of what my Father saw. I am holy and without fault because of Jesus!

Jesus separated us from sin and gave us a brand new identity. When we let that truth penetrate our hearts, peace reigns in us and we rest in the truth that we are qualified for whatever we need because of Jesus! He made us holy! He made us worthy! He made us just like Himself so we can rest in His great love!

Romans 11:16 says, *"If the roots of the tree are holy, the branches will be, too."*

Jesus is the true Vine and we are the branches. We are holy because we are in Him.

In John 15:5,8 Jesus said, *"I am the vine, you are the branches; he who abides in Me and I in him, he bears much fruit, for apart from Me you can do nothing. ⁸My Father is glorified by this, that you bear much fruit, and so prove to be My disciples." NASB*

You are in Jesus and He is in you! What happens in your life when you see yourself as holy because you are one with Jesus?

_____

Jesus told us in these verses that when we live and abide in Him, our lives will bear much fruit! When we see ourselves as holy in Jesus, we live holy lives. Abiding in Jesus is simply believing who you are in Him! Some people believe that if you teach people they are holy and righteous apart from their good works they will live sinful lives. But Jesus taught something quite different. He taught us that the power to live a fruitful life that glorifies your Heavenly Father is found in abiding in Him!

When you teach people that they are holy and without fault because they are in Christ and they believe it, their lives produce righteous fruit! Contrary to what some may think, people don't bear fruit by being put under the Law. Dead works produced by human effort is the result of being under the Law. The only way fruit is produced in our lives is not by our own effort, but by the power of God's Spirit! You are holy not because of what you do; you are holy because of who you are connected to.

Let's end today's study by thanking our Heavenly Father for His gracious gift to us:

Heavenly Father, thank You for loving me and choosing me to be holy and without fault in your eyes! You are my gracious and loving Father and I am so grateful for this free gift You have given me in Jesus!

What was the main truth the Holy Spirit taught you from today's study?

_____

_____

_____

_____

_____

The Gifts of God Are Received by Faith

Romans 11:16-28

Pray before you begin.
Ask the Holy Spirit to reveal Jesus to you in the Scriptures.

Yesterday we learned that our Heavenly Father has declared us holy in Jesus! As we continue reading Romans 11, we will see that the purpose of this chapter of the Bible is to persuade and convince our hearts that the gift of being made holy, righteous and forgiven are received through faith in Jesus!

Romans 11:16-28 *[16] … If the roots of the tree are holy, the branches will be too. [17] But some of these branches from Abraham's tree—some of the people of Israel—have been broken off. And you Gentiles, who were branches from a wild olive tree, have been grafted in. So now you also receive the blessing God has promised Abraham and his children, sharing in the rich nourishment from the root of God's special olive tree. [18] But you must not brag about being grafted in to replace the branches that were broken off. You are just a branch, not the root. [19] "Well," you may say, "those branches were broken off to make room for me." [20] Yes, but remember—those branches were broken off because they didn't believe in Christ, and you are there because you do believe. So don't think highly of yourself, but fear what could happen. NLT [21]*

[21] For if God did not spare the natural branches [because of unbelief], neither will He spare you [if you are guilty of the same offense]. [22] Then note and appreciate the gracious kindness and the severity of God: severity toward those who have fallen, but God's gracious kindness to you — provided you continue in His grace and abide in His kindness; otherwise you too will be cut off (pruned away). AMP

[23] And if the people of Israel turn from their unbelief, they will be grafted in again, for God has the power to graft them back into the tree. [24] You, by nature, were a branch cut from a wild olive tree. So if God was willing to do something contrary to nature by grafting you into His cultivated tree, He will be far more eager to graft the original branches back into the tree where they belong. [25] I

want you to understand this mystery, dear brothers and sisters, so that you will not feel proud about yourselves. Some of the people of Israel have hard hearts, but this will last only until the full number of Gentiles comes to Christ. ²⁶And so all Israel will be saved. As the Scriptures say, "The one who rescues will come from Jerusalem, and he will turn Israel away from ungodliness. ²⁷And this is my covenant with them, that I will take away their sins." ²⁸Many of the people of Israel are now enemies of the Good News, and this benefits you Gentiles. Yet they are still the people he loves because he chose their ancestors Abraham, Isaac, and Jacob. NLT

Look at verse 16, 17, and 27. What three gifts of grace does the Apostle Paul share in these verses that are given to those who have placed their faith in Jesus?

_____

_____

Why were some of the people of Israel not grafted into Jesus? (Verse 20)

_____

Why are you grafted into Jesus? (verse 20)

_____

What will happen to those who do not believe in Jesus, when they begin to believe? (Verse 23)

_____

Where do all of us belong? (verse 24)

_____

How does our Father feel toward those who are enemies of the Good News? (verse 28)

_____

You Are Righteous Through Faith in Jesus!

Romans 11:17 says that those who believe in Jesus have received the blessing promised to Abraham. We learned in Week 1 that the blessing promised to Abraham was the gift of righteousness through Jesus. Let's look at those verses again so we can see clearly what gift of grace the Apostle was talking about in Romans 11:17.

Galatians 3:6-14: *⁶In the same way, "Abraham believed God, and <u>God counted him as righteous because of his faith</u>." ⁷The real children of Abraham, then, are those who put their faith in God. ⁸What's more, the Scriptures looked forward to this time when God would declare the Gentiles to be righteous because of their faith. God proclaimed this good news to Abraham long ago when He said, "All nations will be blessed through you." ⁹<u>So all who put their faith in Christ share the same blessing Abraham received because of his faith</u>. NLT*

¹⁰And all who depend on the Law [who are seeking to be justified by obedience to the Law...] are under a curse and doomed to disappointment and destruction, for it is written in the Scriptures, Cursed be everyone who does not continue to abide by all the precepts and commands written in the Book of the Law and to practice them. AMP

¹¹So it is clear that no one can be made right with God by trying to keep the law. For the Scriptures say, "It is through faith that a righteous person has life." ¹²<u>This way of faith is very different from the way of law</u>, which says, "It is through obeying the law that a person has life." ¹¹But Christ has rescued us from the curse pronounced by the law. When He was hung on the cross, He took upon himself the curse for our wrongdoing. For it is written in the Scriptures, "Cursed is everyone who is hung on a tree." ¹³Through Christ Jesus, <u>God has blessed the Gentiles with the same blessing He promised to Abraham</u>, so that we who are believers might receive the promised Holy Spirit through faith. NLT

What blessing did Abraham receive because of His faith? (verse 6)

_____

So what blessing do we share with Abraham when we place our faith in Christ? (verses 8-9)

_____

_____

Who is doomed to being disappointed? (verse 10) What is made clear? (verse 11)

_____

_____

How can you experience the Life of God? (verse 11)

_____

_____

How is the way of faith different from the way of the law? (verses 12-14)

_____

_____

In this passage of Scripture, we can clearly see that the way of the law is very different from the way of faith.

The way of the law says: "It's through obeying the law that a person will be blessed and have life."

The way of faith says: "Those who depend on their obedience to the law to be blessed by God are under a curse and doomed to disappointment, but those who place their faith in Jesus will receive the blessing promised to Abraham and be made righteous in God's sight!"

Remember that a person must be righteous in order to qualify for the favor and blessing of God, and it's only through faith in Jesus that we will ever be declared righteous! You can never qualify yourself through your perfect obedience to the law. Jesus alone qualifies you.

You Are Forgiven Through Faith in Jesus!

The last gift of grace that the Apostle Paul talks about in Romans 11:16-28 is forgiveness. He reminds us of what the Father promised through Jesus in Romans 11:27: *"And this is My covenant with them, that I will take away their sins."* What Good News to know that our sins are forgiven and we no longer have to live in the guilt and shame of our mistakes! Jesus took away our sins and made us holy in the Father's eyes! We have been given the gift of righteousness because of Jesus!

In Romans 11:16-28 the Apostle Paul emphasizes once again the importance of faith in Jesus! He begins in verse 17 talking about the natural children of Abraham and his natural lineage. He uses the illustration of an olive tree to teach us that even though the children of Israel were natural descendants of Abraham they did not remain in the spiritual lineage because of their unbelief in Christ. Have you ever heard of a family tree? It's an illustration like the one below to show the genealogy of a family.

The Apostle Paul taught us that the natural descendants of Abraham were removed from his spiritual family tree because of their unbelief in Christ, but we who were not natural descendants of Abraham were grafted in because we did believe. In Romans 11:25, he said he wanted us to understand this mystery so that we don't become prideful and begin to think that we are in Christ by some good works of our own. We have been graciously accepted into the lineage of Jesus and have been declared holy, righteous, and forgiven simply through trusting and relying upon Jesus! Romans 11:28 says that even though many of the natural descendants of Abraham are enemies of this Good News, God loves them and it would delight His heart to graft them back in to the family of God! It is the Father's heart that everyone He loves would receive holiness, righteousness and forgiveness through faith in Jesus. Our good works and human effort will never qualify us! Jesus alone qualifies us! We are His beloved children and heirs of His gifts of grace because of Jesus!

What was the main truth the Holy Spirit taught you from today's study?

_____

_____

_____

_____

_____

_____

_____

_____

God's Gifts are Irrevocable

Romans 11:29-35

Pray before you begin.
Ask the Holy Spirit to reveal Jesus to you in the Scriptures.

Today we will finish our study of Romans chapter 11. We will start with a very popular Scripture of the Bible and get a deeper understanding of the truth it teaches.

Romans 11:29: *For God's gifts and His call can never be withdrawn.*

In the KJV this same verse reads: *For the gifts and calling of God are without repentance.*

In order to understand this verse clearly we must remember the context of this Scripture. In Romans 11:16-28 the Apostle Paul tells us of three grace gifts that are given to those who are grafted into Jesus through faith:

• You are made holy through faith in Jesus! (Verse 16)

• You are declared righteous through faith in Jesus! (Verse 17)

• Your sins are taken away through faith in Jesus! (Verse 27)

In preparing for this study, as I read Romans 11:29, everything I had ever been taught about this verse came to my mind. Previously, I had understood this verse to mean that the natural gifts and talents of a person will never be taken away from them even if they do not use them for God's glory. Although there is truth in that statement, it didn't make sense to me how that was the interpretation of this particular Scripture when I read it in context. The Apostle Paul was not talking about the natural talent or natural gifts of a person in this passage. He was teaching us about the gifts of holiness, righteousness and forgiveness that are received only by faith in Jesus.

So what does this verse really mean?

The word *gifts* in this verse comes from the Greek word *charisma* (Strong's G5483). it literally means "deliverance; qualification: a free gift."

The word *call* or *calling* comes from the Greek word *klēsis* (Strong's G2821). It literally means "an invitation."

The word *repentance* in the King James Version or *withdrawn* in the New Living Translation comes from the Greek word *ametamelētos* (Strong's G27). The literal meaning of this Greek word is "irrevocable." *Irrevocable* means it is "irreversible; it can never be taken away once it is given."

So the literal meaning of Romans 11:29 is that the gifts of holiness, righteousness, and forgiveness are irrevocable. They are irreversible and can never be taken away once they are given. The calling or invitation of God to receive His gifts is also irrevocable. That means He will never quit inviting you to receive His gifts of love, and once you do receive them, He will never take them back. Jesus secured your righteousness forever through your faith in Him! You never have to be afraid to lose His gift of salvation! Jesus is your guarantee! Jesus is your qualification! Jesus is your righteousness and He has promised to never leave you nor forsake you! You are safe and secure in His arms forever!

You did not receive His gift of salvation through your good behavior, and you can never lose it by your bad behavior.

> Ephesians 2:8 says: *For it is by free grace (God's unmerited favor) that you are saved (delivered from judgment and made partakers of Christ's salvation) through…faith. And this [salvation] is not of yourselves [not of your own doing, it came not through your own striving], but it is the gift of God. AMP*

It's all about Jesus! Everything comes from Him, lives through Him, and ends in Him!

> Romans 11:30-36: *³⁰Once, you Gentiles were rebels against God, but when the people of Israel rebelled against him, God was merciful to you instead. ³¹Now they are the rebels, and God's mercy has come to you so that they, too, will share in God's mercy. ³²For God has imprisoned everyone in disobedience so he could have mercy on everyone. ³³Oh, how great are God's riches and wisdom and knowledge! How impossible it is for us to understand his decisions and his ways! ³⁴For who can know the LORD's thoughts? Who knows enough to give him advice? ³⁵And who has given him so much that he needs to pay it back? ³⁶For everything comes from him and exists by his power and is intended for his glory. All glory to him forever! Amen.*

What is the heart of the Father toward everyone? (verse 32)

_____

_____

What truth is found in verse 36?

_____

God's standard of holiness is so high that man could never achieve it on his own. So in God's great plan to redeem man, He sent Jesus to be holy in our place. Jesus came from the heart of the Father, died to take the penalty of our sin, rose again to make us righteous, and seated us with Him in Heavenly places. He did this not because of anything we have done to deserve it, but to clearly demonstrate the immeasurable riches of His grace in His kindness and goodness of heart toward us in Christ Jesus (Ephesians 2:6-7). The law showed us all that we needed a Savior and that He alone can qualify us! Everything comes from Him, lives through Him, and ends in Him! All glory goes to Him! And because of His great love for us, He shared His glory with us all! (John 17:22)

Let's end today's study by reading Romans 11:32-36 out of the Message Bible:

>*³²In one way or another, God makes sure that we all experience what it means to be outside so that he can personally open the door and welcome us back in. ³³Have you ever come on anything quite like this extravagant generosity of God, this deep, deep wisdom? It's way over our heads. We'll never figure it out. ³⁴Is there anyone around who can explain God? ³⁵Anyone smart enough to tell him what to do ³Anyone who has done him such a huge favor that God has to ask his advice? ³⁶Everything comes from him; Everything happens through him; Everything ends up in him. Always glory! Always praise! Yes. Yes. Yes. MSG*

So Awake to Righteousness

Jesus alone qualifies you! You have been made holy, righteous, and forgiven, not through any works of your own, but through faith in Jesus alone! Your salvation is secure! You never have to fear losing any of the gifts God has given you because His free gifts are irrevocable! They are irreversible! They will never be taken back once they are given. You belong to Jesus forever and nothing or no one will ever snatch you out of His hand! His heart is merciful and kind toward you and nothing could ever separate you from His great love!

What was the main truth the Holy Spirit taught you from today's study?

_____
_____
_____
_____

Let God Transform the Way You Think

Romans 12

Day 1

Grace — God's Divine Influence Upon Your Mind

Day 2

We Are Equal in Christ

Day 3

The Fruit of Righteousness

Grace — God's Divine Influence Upon Your Mind

Romans 12:1-2

Pray before you begin.
Ask the Holy Spirit to reveal Jesus to you in the Scriptures.

In Romans 11 the Apostle Paul teaches that we receive the truth that we are holy, righteous, and forgiven through faith in Christ. In Romans chapter 12:1-2, he begins by appealing to us, based on the mercy God has shown toward us, to make a conscious decision to present ourselves before God as a living sacrifice. Today we will learn what that means and how to apply it in our lives.

Romans 12:1-2: *¹I appeal to you therefore, brethren, and beg of you in view of [all] the mercies of God, to make a decisive dedication of your bodies [presenting all your members and faculties] as a living sacrifice, holy (devoted, consecrated) and well pleasing to God, which is your reasonable service and spiritual worship. ²Do not be conformed to this world (this age), [fashioned after and adapted to its external, superficial customs], but be transformed (changed) by the [entire] renewal of your mind [by its new ideals and its new attitude], so that you may prove [for yourselves] what is the good and acceptable and perfect will of God, even the thing which is good and acceptable and perfect [in His sight for you]. AMP*

What is the Apostle Paul strongly encouraging you to do in verse 1?

_____

What does he mean by presenting yourself as a living sacrifice? What does He want you to believe about yourself? (verse 1)

_____

_____

_____

Why is it important for your mind to be renewed to the truth that you are holy and well-pleasing to God? Why does your Heavenly Father want your mind to be renewed by this truth? (verse 2)

_____

_____

Over the past few weeks, we have been learning a great deal about righteousness and grace. We learned that the word *grace* comes from the Greek word *charis* and it means "good will, loving-kindness, favour; the merciful kindness by which God, exerting his holy influence upon souls, turns them to Christ, and keeps, strengthens, and increases them in Christian faith" (Strong's 5485, BLB). Your soul is your mind, will, and emotions. Grace is the merciful kindness by which God exerts His holy influence upon your mind and helps you to keep your mind focused on Jesus and empowers you to trust and rely upon Him! The Spirit of Grace transforms your thoughts by persuading your heart that you are holy, righteous and well-pleasing to God because of Jesus!

Present Yourself as a Living Sacrifice

Do you want your life to honor and glorify God? In the Amplified Bible, Jude 1:24 says that Jesus presents you before the Father as holy, blameless and without fault with ecstatic delight! The Father and the Son are pleased with you! Here in Roman 12:1 the Apostle Paul is appealing to you to present yourself the same way that Jesus does. He begs you to present yourself holy, righteous, consecrated, and well-pleasing before God as a living sacrifice, for this is true worship. This is how you truly honor and glorify God by acknowledging what Jesus has done for you!

Let's look at Romans 12:1 in the Message Bible:

> Romans 12:1: *So here's what I want you to do, God helping you: Take your everyday, ordinary life — your sleeping, eating, going-to-work, and walking-around life — and place it before God as an offering. Embracing what God does for you is the best thing you can do for him. MSG*

Embracing what Jesus has done for you — believing the truth that He made you holy and well-pleasing to the Father — is the best thing you can do for God. We have often thought that sacrificing our lives for Jesus had to do with our actions, but in truth it has to do with our heart. When you truly embrace what He has done for you and who you are in Him, the fruit of love, joy, peace and kindness will flow from your heart effortlessly by the power of His Spirit. Your actions will be the fruit of what you believe is true about you!

When you give a gift to someone, how do you want them to respond? Don't you simply want to see the smile on their face when they open it? Doesn't it bring your heart joy when they simply receive it with a thankful heart? If I was to give someone I love a birthday present and they looked at me and said, "Now, what can I do for you?" That wouldn't be the best thing they could do for me. The best thing they could do for me would be to simply embrace what I did for them! I would want them to simply receive and enjoy what I gave them as my gift of love.

So what does presenting yourself as a living sacrifice to God look like in real life? It is embracing what He has done for you! I often talk to the Father about how thankful I am for all He has done for me. I say, "Father, I know You love me! Thank You for giving me the gift of righteousness through Jesus! It brings me such peace to know that You are pleased with me, and I am perfect and without fault in Your sight! You are good and loving and I am just like You!" This is what it looks like to present yourself to the Father as a living sacrifice; for you are giving up your negative opinion of yourself for His good opinion of you!

Let God Transform the Way You Think

In Romans 12:2 we see the Apostle Paul admonishing us to not be conformed to the world, but be transformed by the renewing of our minds. The way the world thinks and the way Jesus thinks are quite different. The world is all about performance and who can make it to the top first. The world's way of thinking is that some people are more important and valuable than others and your worth is found in what you do. But the way Jesus thinks is that He provided the sacrifice necessary for every person to sit in the top position — seated with Him in heavenly places. He showed us that everyone is equally important, valuable, and loved. And He made us holy and well-pleasing to the Father by giving us the gift of righteousness!

Grace is the very power to transform the way you think. For many years of my Christian life my thinking was not right. My mind was often filled with feelings of lack and inadequacy. My thoughts were often filled with comparisons and judgments. I thought I was better than some people, and not as good as others. I had a worldly way of thinking even though I was a child of God. Even when I recognized that my thoughts were wrong, I still thought it was my responsibility to change the way I was thinking. True renewal of my mind never occurred until I began to understand grace. Grace is the power of the Holy Spirit at work in me. Philippians 2:13 says, *[Not in your own strength] for it is God Who is all the while effectually at work in you [energizing and creating in you the power and desire], both to will and to work for His good pleasure and satisfaction and delight. AMP* True transformation does not come by trying hard to think positive, which is just the world's way of trying to keep good thoughts in your mind. Positive thinking is good, but it is still something that you are doing in your own human effort.

When you start trying to transform your own mind by positive thinking, you may have some success with it. But if you are doing it in your own strength, you may get a little prideful about it. You might think about someone else who is struggling and think, "Well, if they'd just change the way they think, their lives would be like mine." If we do not understand that we live and move and have our being in Jesus, we end up in self-effort and self-reliance and being judgmental of everyone who has not accomplished as much as we have. But if we will remember that true transformation comes by God's grace, we can encourage others that they don't have to change the way they think by themselves. Jesus will help them. For in our weakness, He makes us strong! (2 Corinthians 12:9).

When I was a young girl, I accepted Jesus as my Savior, but it wasn't until I was in my mid 20s that I began to experience being transformed by the renewing of my mind. This is because I discovered the mystery of the Gospel, and it's *Christ in me, the hope of glory* (Colossians 1:27). Only in Christ and only through His strength, can I truly think correctly. When negative, lying thoughts have bombarded my mind, it was only by His power and strength, that I could feel my thoughts and perspective changing. Simply by acknowledging, "Father, I am thinking wrong. I need your grace right now to think like You!" When you learn to live like that, your life is truly transformed by the power of God's Spirit!

Romans 12:2 tells us to be transformed by the renewing of our minds so that we can experience the good, acceptable, and perfect will of God for our lives. The will of God for your life begins in your heart. It's not His will for you to be fearful, worried, upset, angry, or resentful toward someone. The will of God is that you experience peace, joy, love, goodness, and kindness in your heart.

As you invite God's spirit into your thoughts, what changes first is the way you see the Father, and then, how you see yourself. And as you begin to see yourself as righteous, holy, acceptable and well-pleasing to God, the way you see others begins to change as well. There have been many times when I could feel the Spirit of God helping me to think correctly. When I was upset, frustrated, fearful or worried, I needed God's grace to come in and transform the way I thought, so that I could experience His will in my life. Proverbs 4:23 tells us to "guard our thoughts with all diligence, for they determine the course of our lives." The way we think determines the fruit of our lives.

Let me share an example of how the Holy Spirit helps to transform our thoughts. A particular situation had arisen where I had to correct my son because he had not made a wise decision. Usually when I correct my children, I will go to the Lord and He will give me peace and wisdom, and He will help me handle it correctly. This time, I found myself getting very upset with the situation, because it was the fourth time I had come to him for the same thing. In frustration, I told him how he had done wrong, and that he needed to make wiser choices. As I was talking to him, he looked at me strangely, because the way I was talking to him was not the way I normally talk to him. When I was finished, he looked at me and said, "Mom, you are not seeing me the way God sees me." Realizing that he was correct and that my thoughts were not filled with grace, I took a deep breath, and replied, "I'll be right back." I walked away from the situation, called out to Jesus and prayed, "Jesus. I need your grace, today. I am not thinking correctly, and I need Your grace right now to help me." I realized I had let fear into my heart concerning this situation, and I needed His love to set me free! So I sat down and let Him minister His love to me and wash over my mind. As I listened, His grace influenced my heart and changed the way I was thinking. He reminded me that it was His grace that creates the desire and power in my child's heart to do His will, and that the law could never change him. No amount of frustration, being upset and angry, or pointing out his faults was going to change him. Only the power of His grace — knowing and believing who he is in Christ — has the power to transform his mind and change his life.

I stayed in that room with the Lord, until my mind was renewed. Then I walked back out to my son, and said, "You are right. I wasn't seeing you the way that God sees you. But you know what, you're not seeing yourself the way God sees you either." He looked at me and said, "You are right, Mom." Then we began to talk about what God says about him, and who he is in Christ, and about God's great plan for Him. In that situation, when I invited the Holy Spirit into my thought process, He not only changed the way I was thinking, but He changed the way my son was thinking too. And I saw God's will come to pass in that area of his life. It is grace that transforms the way we think, and it is grace that brings to pass the good, acceptable, and perfect will of God in our lives.

Let's take a look at Romans 12:2 in two other translations of the Bible:

> *Fix your attention on God. You'll be changed from the inside out. MSG*

> *Don't copy the behavior and customs of this world, but <u>let God transform you into a new person by changing the way you think.</u> Then you will learn to know God's will for you, which is good and pleasing and perfect.*

And Ephesians 4:23-24 says, *[23]Let the Spirit renew your thoughts and attitudes. [24]Put on your new nature, created to be like God—truly righteous and holy.*

Let the Spirit renew your thoughts and attitudes. When you feel your heart experiencing negative emotions, fix your eyes on Jesus! Present yourself as a living sacrifice, holy and acceptable to Him. His grace influences our mind, will and emotions and brings peace to our soul. The renewing of our minds is not a human effort to try to think right, but rather a work of God's Spirit that happens as we look to Him for the grace to transform our hearts and lives. It's all about a relationship with the One who loves us and empowers us to be everything He created us to be.

In every situation, simply invite Jesus into your thought process. Let Him change the way you see Him, yourself, and others, and ultimately your circumstances. Even though you have your Father's heart and the mind of Christ, it is the Spirit that brings it out in your life. As you look to Him, ask Him to do this work in you, and you will find yourself thinking like Jesus. As your heart becomes convinced of His great love for you, you will experience His good and perfect will for every area of your life! You will be transformed by the entire renewal of your mind

What was the main truth the Holy Spirit taught you from today's study?

_____

_____

_____

_____

_____

_____

_____

_____

We Are Equal in Christ

Romans 12:3-9

Pray before you begin.
Ask the Holy Spirit to reveal Jesus to you in the Scriptures.

Yesterday we studied Romans 12:1-2. Verse 1 taught us to present ourselves before God as holy, consecrated, and well-pleasing to Him. Verse 2 admonished us to not think like the world, but to let God transform us by changing the way we think, so that we can experience His perfect will for our lives. The Apostle Paul then goes on, in Roman 12:3-9, to teach us how God thinks about us. Today we will invite the Holy Spirit to change the way we think about each other and realize that we are all equally valuable and important in the body of Christ.

Let's read Romans 12:3-9 in the Amplified Bible:

> ³For by the grace (unmerited favor of God) given to me I warn everyone among you not to estimate and think of himself more highly than he ought [not to have an exaggerated opinion of his own importance], but to rate his ability with sober judgment, each according to the degree of faith apportioned by God to him. ⁴For as in one physical body we have many parts (organs, members) and all of these parts do not have the same function or use, ⁵So we, numerous as we are, are one body in Christ (the Messiah) and individually we are parts one of another [mutually dependent on one another]. ⁶Having gifts (faculties, talents, qualities) that differ according to the grace given us, let us use them: [He whose gift is] prophecy, [let him prophesy] according to the proportion of his faith; ⁷[He whose gift is] practical service, let him give himself to serving; he who teaches, to his teaching; ⁸He who exhorts (encourages), to his exhortation; he who contributes, let him do it in simplicity and liberality; he who gives aid and superintends, with zeal and singleness of mind; he who does acts of mercy, with genuine cheerfulness and joyful eagerness. ⁹[Let your] love be sincere (a real thing); hate what is evil [loathe all ungodliness, turn in horror from wickedness], but hold fast to that which is good. AMP

Now let's look at Romans 12:3-9 in the Message Bible:

> *3 "I'm speaking to you out of deep gratitude for all that God has given me, and especially as I have responsibilities in relation to you. Living then, as every one of you does, in pure grace, it's important that you not misinterpret yourselves as people who are bringing this goodness to God. No, God brings [the goodness] to you. The only accurate way to understand ourselves is by what God is and by what he does for us, not by what we are and what we do for him. 4 In this way we are like the various parts of a human body. Each part gets its meaning from the body as a whole, not the other way around. 5 The body we're talking about is Christ's body of chosen people. Each of us finds our meaning and function as a part of his body. But as a chopped-off finger or cut-off toe we wouldn't amount to much, would we? So since we find ourselves fashioned into all these excellently formed and marvelously functioning parts in Christ's body, 6 let's just go ahead and be what we were made to be, <u>without enviously or pridefully comparing ourselves with each other, or trying to be something we aren't.</u> If you preach, just preach God's Message, nothing else; 7 if you help, just help, don't take over; if you teach, stick to your teaching; 8 if you give encouraging guidance, be careful that you don't get bossy; if you're put in charge, don't manipulate; if you're called to give aid to people in distress, keep your eyes open and be quick to respond; if you work with the disadvantaged, don't let yourself get irritated with them or depressed by them. Keep a smile on your face. 9 Love from the center of who you are. MSG*

How does God want you to think of yourself in relation to others? (verse 3, AMP)

_____

_____

What does the Apostle Paul encourage you to live in? How does the Message Bible explain what it means to live in grace? (verse 3)

_____

_____

As the Body of Christ, why are we all equally valuable and important? (verses 4-5, MSG)

_____

_____

Each one of us has been gifted by God's grace, what does verse 6 in the message Bible teach us about comparing ourselves to others?

_____

According to Romans 12:6-8, what are the seven grace gifts that the Holy Spirit gives to the body of Christ?

_____ _____ _____

_____ _____ _____ _____

Where does verse 9 in the Message Bible encourage us to love from?

_____

Romans 12:3 tells us to not think of ourselves more highly than someone else, but rather to think of ourselves according to the grace that God has given us in Christ. In Romans 12:2 the Apostle Paul taught us to not be conformed to this world, but to be transformed by the renewing of our minds. The world's way of thinking is to judge people based on their behavior, their talent, or their social status. This causes a person to judge themselves better or worse than someone else based on our performance, but that's not how the Father judges us. He judges us based on the performance of Jesus and His finished work. His grace persuades our hearts that we are all equally loved by Him! Grace teaches us to see each other as one in Jesus. We are all part of the body of Christ and equally valuable and important no matter what are gifts are. We are all equal in Christ — holy, acceptable, and well-pleasing to the Father!

Romans 12:6 in the Message Bible encourages us to be what we were made to be, without being envious or prideful, and without comparing ourselves to each other, or trying to be something that we are not.

Have you ever been tempted to be envious or prideful in comparing yourself to someone else? Can you think of a recent example?

_____

_____

How can we overcome the temptation to compare ourselves with each other?

_____

I know there have been times that I have been tempted to be envious or prideful in comparing myself to others, thinking I was better or worse than someone else. I can remember looking at one of my close friends who had the beautiful gift of hospitality and thinking, "Why can't I be like her? She is so good at entertaining and putting together a party for others to enjoy. Everyone loves her!" Every time I've been tempted to compare myself to someone it was because I lost sight of Jesus and began to judge based on the world's standards of value. But I want to live out of who I am Christ, not out of the world's judgments and opinions of me. I know it is only by God's grace that I can see myself and others as equal in Christ. So when comparisons and judgments try to arise in my heart, I turn my thoughts to Jesus and invite Him into my thought process. I say, "Jesus, I need your grace. Help me to see myself and others through Your eyes." When I ask Him to help me in this way, He always persuades my heart that we are all equally valuable in Him. Our value does not come from what we do or how gifted we are or how much people like us. Our value is found in the price Jesus paid for us!

We are all uniquely gifted and are all equally important. In Romans 12:6-8 the Apostle Paul describes the different gifts God has given to the body of Christ. These verses describe seven grace gifts given by the Holy Spirit. They include:

1. Prophecy
2. Helping
3. Teaching
4. Encouraging
5. Administration
6. Giving
7. Acts of Compassion

Each of these gifts is equally important and all of them are needed for the body of Christ to function as God intended it to. As God's grace works in our hearts, we can truly love ourselves as God's wonderful masterpiece, enjoying the gift God has given us while still appreciating the gift He has given to others.

As you embrace who you are in Jesus, you will find yourself living free from envy or pride in comparing yourself to others. As your mind is renewed to the truth that every single one of us is uniquely gifted by the grace of God and equally valuable, you'll begin to see yourself and others through the Father's eyes. When you see a person operating in their gift, you are seeing the glory of God in them. Every gift that we have been given has come from the character and nature of God, and none is more important than the other. All of our gifts are needed to function together as one body as we display God's glory in the earth. So awake to righteousness, and appreciate the unique masterpiece that you are, wonderfully made in the image of God, and gifted by His grace to display His glory in the world! Love from the center of who you are!

What was the main truth the Holy Spirit taught you from today's study?

_____

_____

_____

_____

The Fruit of Righteousness

Romans 12:9-21

Pray before you begin.
Ask the Holy Spirit to reveal Jesus to you in the Scriptures.

Today we will finish our study of Romans chapter 12 looking at verses 12:9-21 in the light of Jesus.

As we awake to righteousness, and allow God's grace to change the way we think about ourselves, the fruit of righteousness will manifest in our lives through the power of God's Spirit. Romans 12 began with Paul appealing to us to present ourselves to God as holy, consecrated, and well pleasing to Him, for this is true worship. He encouraged us to not conform to this world's way of thinking, but to let God transform us by changing the way we think. Then He goes on to teach us about the fruit of righteousness. As you read through these last verses of Romans chapter 12, remember that Jesus made you righteous. These verses reveal your new nature in Him! This fruit does not come out in your life by you trying harder or depending on your ability to change yourself. It comes by you relying upon Jesus and inviting Him to change the way you think. As we rely upon Him, the fruit of righteousness will come out of our lives by the power of His grace! We will love out of the center of who we are! Grace gives us the power to live a righteous life!

Romans 12:9: *Love from the center of who you are! MSG*

Romans 12:9-21: *⁹[Let your] love be sincere (a real thing); hate what is evil… but hold fast to that which is good. ¹⁰Love one another with brotherly affection [as members of one family], giving precedence and showing honor to one another. ¹¹Never lag in zeal and in earnest endeavor; be aglow and burning with the Spirit, serving the Lord. ¹²Rejoice and exult in hope; be steadfast and patient in suffering and tribulation; be constant in prayer. ¹³Contribute to the needs of God's people [sharing in the necessities of the saints]; pursue the practice of hospitality. ¹⁴Bless those who persecute you [who are cruel in their attitude toward you]; bless and do not curse them. ¹⁵Rejoice with those who rejoice [sharing others' joy], and weep with those who weep [sharing others' grief]. ¹⁶Live in harmony with one another; do not be haughty (snobbish, high-*

minded, exclusive), but readily adjust yourself to [people, things] and give yourselves to humble tasks. Never overestimate yourself or be wise in your own conceits. ¹⁷Repay no one evil for evil, but take thought for what is honest and proper and noble [aiming to be above reproach] in the sight of everyone. ¹⁸If possible, as far as it depends on you, live at peace with everyone. ¹⁹Beloved, never avenge yourselves but leave the way open for [God's] wrath; for it is written, Vengeance is Mine, I will repay, says the Lord. ²⁰But if your enemy is hungry, feed him; if he is thirsty, give him drink; for by so doing you will heap burning coals upon his head. ²¹Do not let yourself be overcome by evil, but overcome evil with good. AMP

Remember it's the Spirit of Grace that brings out the fruit of righteousness in our lives. Read back over each verse and describe what the fruit of righteousness looks like.

Verse 9: _____

Verse 10: _____

Verse 11: _____

Verse 12: _____

Verse 13: _____

Verse 14: _____

Verse 15: _____

Verse 16: _____

Verse 17: _____

Verse 18: _____

Verse 19: _____

Verses 20 and 21: _____

Read Romans 12:1-2 from Day 1 of this week's study. How does this fruit of righteousness come out in your life?

_____

Romans 12:9-21 reveals what the fruit of righteousness looks like in our lives. According to these verses, the fruit of righteousness is hating evil and holding fast to that which is good. It's loving and honoring one another and joyfully serving the Lord. It's rejoicing in hope, being patient when you are in a trial, and staying in constant fellowship with Jesus. It's giving to those in need and opening your home to be a blessing to others. The fruit of righteousness is blessing those who do you wrong, rejoicing with those who rejoice, and weeping with those who weep. It's living in harmony and peace with others, and not thinking more highly of yourself than someone else. The fruit of righteousness comes out in our lives and we experience God's will for us by renewing our mind to who we are in Christ. By inviting the Spirit of Grace into our thought process, our hearts are transformed, and love, joy and peace is the fruit of our lives. As who we are on the inside comes out for the whole world to see, our lives will glorify our Heavenly Father.

Let's take a closer took at Romans 12:19-21 as we end today's study:

> Romans 12:19-21: ¹⁹Beloved, do not <u>avenge</u> yourselves, but rather give place to wrath; for it is written, "<u>Vengeance</u> is Mine, I will repay," says the Lord. ²⁰Therefore "If your enemy is hungry, feed him; If he is thirsty, give him a drink; For in so doing you will <u>heap coals of fire</u> on his head." ²¹Do not be overcome by evil, but overcome evil with good. *NKJV*

If one reads theses verses without a clear understanding of the Father's heart, it looks like the Apostle Paul is teaching us that we don't need to take revenge on someone who has done us wrong because our Father will take revenge for us. But in Luke 6:35 Jesus teaches us to treat our enemies the way our Heavenly Father treats the wicked. In this verse, Jesus said, *"Love your enemies! Do good to them. Lend to them without expecting to be repaid. Then your reward from heaven will be very great, and you will truly be acting as children of the Most High, for he is kind and merciful to those who are unthankful and wicked."*

How does your loving Heavenly Father treat the unthankful and wicked?

_____

With this in mind, let's look deeper into the Greek words found in Romans 12:19 to reveal what the Apostle Paul was really teaching us in these verses.

The word *avenge* in verse 19 comes from the Greek word *ekdikeō* (Strong's G1556). It means: "to vindicate one's right; do one justice; to protect, defend, one person from another."

Vengeance in verse 19 comes from the Greek word *ekdikēsis* (Strong's G1557). According to *Marvin Vincent Word Studies in the New Testament*, it "carries with it a sense of vindication" as described in Luke 18:7-8. So to get a clearer understanding of the truth being taught in Romans 12:19, let's look at what Jesus taught us about the Father in Luke 18:7-8: *7And will not [our just] God defend and protect and avenge His elect (His chosen ones), who cry to Him day and night? Will He defer them and delay help on their behalf? 8I tell you, He will defend and protect and avenge them speedily. AMP*

With these definitions in mind, we can clearly understand what the Apostle Paul is teaching us in Romans 12:19-21. Have you ever been treated badly or judged wrongly, and wanted to defend yourself? Have you ever felt angry and wanted to get back at a person who has done you wrong in some way? That is the natural response we have all felt when evil is done to us. We want to make sure that people don't think we are bad; that we aren't being taken advantage of; and that we don't lose out in some way. The natural response is to defend, protect, and avenge ourselves. But the Apostle Paul was teaching us a better way to live! He begins verse 19 by reminding us that we are, "Beloved." We are dearly loved and the Father wants to take care of every concern of our heart. He tells us you don't have to defend, protect, or avenge yourself because the Father has promised to defend, protect, and vindicate you!

> Isaiah 54:17 says: *But no weapon that is formed against you shall prosper, and every tongue that shall rise against you in judgment you shall show to be in the wrong. This [peace, righteousness, security, triumph over opposition] is the heritage of the servants of the Lord [those in whom the ideal Servant of the Lord is reproduced]; this is the righteousness or the vindication which they obtain from Me [this is that which I impart to them as their justification], says the Lord. AMP*

Vindication from the Lord is your inheritance as a dearly loved, righteous child of God. When you know who you are, you don't have to protect or defend yourself. You don't have to attack somebody who's attacking you. You don't have to prove that you are right. Jesus has made you right. Leave the situation in your Father's hands and He'll make all things right for you.

The story of Joseph is a perfect example of this. He was betrayed by his own family, misjudged by those he worked for, and thrown in prison for something he didn't do. He was treated badly by those around him, but He trusted God to vindicate and defend him. In the end, the Father not only vindicated and blessed Joseph by exalting him to second in command, He also restored everything that had been taken from him. And He worked through Joseph to bless and provide for the very ones who had done him wrong. Joseph knew he was loved by the Father and he trusted his heart and life to Him, and as a result he was not overcome by evil, but He overcame evil with good! He experienced the good, acceptable, and perfect will of God for His life!

When we have been treated badly, the temptation is great to avenge and defend ourselves, but this will only bring fear, anger and anxiety into our lives. True peace is found when we trust our hearts and lives to our Father who loves us and will defend, protect, and vindicate us in every situation. When your heart is filled with anger, hurt, or resentment toward someone, invite the Spirit of grace into your thought process. You can't change yourself, but you will be transformed by asking Jesus to help you! Let the Spirit of Grace change the way you think, and you will experience the good, acceptable, and perfect will of God for your life!

So Awake to Righteousness and let the Spirit renew your mind to Who you are in Christ!

Father, thank You for empowering me to love from the center of who I am. You made me righteous and I trust You to bring out righteous fruit in my life. By Your Grace, I am empowered to hate what is evil, and to hold fast to that which is good. You have empowered me to bring honor to others, to rejoice in hope, be patient during trials, and to live in constant fellowship with You. Because I have your nature, I give to those in need and share my home with others. I bless those who have hurt me. I rejoice with those who rejoice and weep with those who weep. I live in harmony with others; I don't think more highly of myself than anyone else, and I give myself to humble tasks. With Your help, I will not repay evil for evil, but I live at peace with others. I don't have to justify or defend myself when others have treated me unfairly because I know You will vindicate and defend me! I am not overcome by evil, but I overcome evil with good because I am just like Jesus in this world! Thank You for helping me change the way I think and bear righteous fruit so that I can enjoy Your good, acceptable and perfect will for my life!

What was the main truth the Holy Spirit taught you from today's study?

_____

_____

_____

_____

_____

_____

_____

_____

Clothe Yourself with Jesus

Romans 13

Day 1

Respect for Authority

Day 2

Love from the Center of Who You Are

Day 3

Awake to Righteousness

Respect for Authority

Romans 13:1-7

Pray before you begin.
Ask the Holy Spirit to reveal Jesus to you in the Scriptures.

Today we will continue to renew our minds to who we are in Christ. We will see what righteous fruit looks like in our lives. In the first 11 chapters of Romans, the Apostle Paul reiterated the truth that we are made righteous — not by our good works — but by God's grace. We will never be made righteous in God's sight through our obedience to the law. We were declared righteous when we placed our faith in Jesus! In Romans, chapters 12-16, he begins to instruct us in righteous living. He teaches us about our new nature in Christ. In this lesson, we will learn that respect for authority is a righteous fruit that will come out in our lives when we believe who we are in Jesus!

Romans 13:1-7: *¹Everyone must submit to governing authorities. For all authority comes from God, and those in positions of authority have been placed there by God. ²So anyone who rebels against authority is rebelling against what God has instituted, and they will be punished. ³For the authorities do not strike fear in people who are doing right, but in those who are doing wrong. Would you like to live without fear of the authorities? Do what is right, and they will honor you. ⁴The authorities are God's servants, <u>sent for your good</u>. But if you are doing wrong, of course you should be afraid, for they have the power to punish you. They are God's servants, sent for the very purpose of punishing those who do what is wrong. ⁵So you must submit to them, not only to avoid punishment, but also to keep a clear conscience. ⁶Pay your taxes, too, for these same reasons. For government workers need to be paid. They are serving God in what they do. ⁷Give to everyone what you owe them: Pay your taxes and government fees to those who collect them, and give respect and honor to those who are in authority.*

What righteous instruction does the Apostle Paul give in Romans 13:1-2?

_____

_____

How can you live without fear of those who God has placed in authority? (verse 3)

_____

Why were governing authorities sent by God? (verse 4)

_____

What righteous instruction does the Apostle Paul give to us in Romans 13:5-7?

_____

_____

In this passage of Scripture, we are given righteous instruction to obey the law of the land, pay our taxes, and honor and respect those who are in authority. Our loving Heavenly Father has placed authorities in the world for our good. The law of the land is set up to protect us. As long as the laws of the land do not violate God's law, we as righteous children of God respect that authority and obey the laws set in place. We don't obey them to make ourselves righteous, but because that is our new nature in Christ.

Throughout history, unrighteous leaders have oppressed the people they were governing. During these times when God's people have prayed for justice, they were vindicated and set free from their oppressors. As the Scriptures say, we will live in fear if we do not obey the law of the land because we know that those who break the law are punished for their wrong behavior. However, we never have to be afraid of standing up for what is good and right even if it opposes those in authority. We see this truth very clearly in the story of Daniel and the lion's den. The governing officials had created a law that said the people could only pray to the ruling king. But Daniel did not submit to that law because he was submitting to a higher authority — he prayed to the King of kings! As a result, even though the governing officials threw him into the lion's den, God vindicated and protected him. He delivered Daniel from his oppressors and showed His glory to the people of that land because Daniel had put his trust in God!

As righteous children of God, we have been given great power and authority to effect change in our world. We have the Spirit of Grace at work in us empowering us with courage and faith to trust God with those who govern over us.

1 Timothy 2:1-4: _¹I urge you, first of all, to pray for all people. Ask God to help them; intercede on their behalf, and give thanks for them. ²Pray this way for kings and all who are in authority so that we can live peaceful and quiet lives marked by godliness and dignity. ³This is good and pleases God our Savior, ⁴who wants everyone to be saved and to understand the truth._

What does 1 Timothy 2:1 instruct us to do as righteous children of God?

_____

What will this produce in our lives? (verse 2)

_____

How does God feel about your prayers for governing officials? (verses 3-4)

_____

First Timothy 2:1-2 instructs us to pray for those who are in authority over us so that we can live peaceful and quiet lives marked by godliness and dignity. It pleases our Father when we trust Him with those governing over us because it is His will that everyone would be saved and come to know the truth. Proverbs 21:1 says, *"The king's heart is in the hand of the LORD, like the rivers of water; He turns it wherever He wishes. NKJV* As children of God, we can rest, assured that our Heavenly Father is the King of all kings and He can turn any king's heart in the direction of his will. When we ask Him to bring His will to pass, our prayers will be powerful and effective because He has made us righteous in Christ Jesus! (James 5:16)

Let's end today's study by praying for those who govern over us:

Heavenly Father, thank You for making me righteous and instructing me in the ways of righteousness. I respect those who are in authority over me and obey the law of the land because that is who I am in You! Give me the courage to always stand for what is true and right, and help me to trust You with those in authority! Today I pray for all the governing officials in our nation. I ask that You exert Your Holy influence upon their hearts and turn them in the direction of Your will. I pray for righteous and godly leaders to rise up in our nation and for Your will to be done in the hearts of men. I thank You that I can live the peaceful and quiet life You promised when I pray for those in authority, and place my trust in You! You are the King of kings and I pray Your will be done in the earth! Thank You for manifesting Your glory in the earth! In Jesus' Name, Amen

What was the main truth the Holy Spirit taught you from today's study?

_____

_____

_____

_____

_____

Love from the Center of Who You Are

Romans 13:8-10

Pray before you begin.
Ask the Holy Spirit to reveal Jesus to you in the Scriptures.

Today we will study Romans 13:8-10. In these verses, we will learn that love is the fruit of righteousness! God is Love! Since we are His children, we have His DNA. We are love because we are loved! (1 John 4:19) Love is who we are and it flows from our hearts as we renew our minds to the truth that we have been made righteous in Jesus!

> Romans 13:8-10: *⁸Owe nothing to anyone—except for your obligation to love one another. If you love your neighbor, you will fulfill the requirements of God's law. ⁹For the commandments say, "You must not commit adultery. You must not murder. You must not steal. You must not covet." These — and other such commandments — are summed up in this one commandment: "Love your neighbor as yourself." ¹⁰Love does no wrong to others, so love fulfills the requirements of God's law.*

Which commandment sums up all of God's commands? (verse 9)

_____

Why does the command to love fulfill the requirements of God's law? (verse 10)

_____

We must remember that it's not obeying the command to love that makes us righteous before God, but when our hearts are established in the truth that Jesus made us righteous, love will be the fruit of our lives! Love is the fruit of trusting and relying upon Jesus!

> Colossians 3:9-14: *You have stripped off your old evil nature and all its wicked deeds. ¹⁰In its place you have clothed yourself with a brand new nature that is continually being renewed as you learn more about Christ, who created this new nature within you. ¹¹In this new life, it doesn't matter if you are a Jew or a*

Gentile…. Christ is all that matters, and he lives in all of us. [12]Since God chose you to be the holy people who he loves, clothe yourselves with tenderhearted mercy, kindness, humility, gentleness and patience. [13]You must make allowance for each other's faults and forgive the person who offends you. Remember, the Lord forgave you, so you [can] forgive others. [14]And the most important piece of clothing you must wear is love.

What has been stripped from you and what has been put in its place? (verses 9-10)

_____

_____

In your new life, what is the only thing that really matters? (verse 11)

_____

What did God choose you to be? (verse 12)

_____

What is your new nature in Christ? What will be the fruit of our lives when we embrace the truth that we are chosen, holy, and loved? (verse 12)

_____

_____

Why do you have the power to forgive those who have hurt you? (verse 13)

_____

What is the most important piece of clothing that you wear? (verse 14)

_____

The Apostle Paul admonished us in Romans 13:9 to love from the center of who we are! It's only when we believe the truth that we are dearly loved and forgiven in Jesus, that we have the power to truly love and forgive others. Colossians 3:9-14 teaches us that we no longer have an evil nature, we have been given a brand new nature that is just like Jesus! The more we learn about who we are in Jesus, the more of this new nature comes out in our lives.

Colossians 3:12 says that God chose you to be holy and dearly loved. When you realize and embrace that truth, the fruit of mercy, kindness, gentleness, humility, and patience will flow effortlessly from your heart toward others. It is simply who you are! We are empowered to forgive those who have offended us when we remember that we are forgiven! Colossians 3:14 says that the most important piece of clothing we must wear is Love! Love does no wrong to anyone, so it is the fulfillment of God's law. God's law is holy, just and good and we have been made holy, just and good because of Jesus (Romans 7:12; Romans 3:22-24). When we daily rely upon Him, love will be the righteous fruit of our lives.

Let me share a personal example from my own life. There have been many times in my life when people have said evil things about me. Especially, since I am a teacher of the Good News, there are those who disagree and therefore want to discredit me. On one of those particular occasions I received a phone call from a lady who was very unhappy with me because of what I taught.

She proceeded too tell me how I was teaching error and if I didn't change what I was teaching she was going to let people know that they should not listen to what I teach.

As she was talking, I turned my thoughts to the Father and said, "Father, I need Your help!" I was tempted to defend myself and worry about what she thought, but as I invited the Spirit of Grace into my mind and heart, I felt a peace come over me. I actually felt the Father smiling down on me and reminding me that He loved me and I was safe in His love and approval. The natural way to respond when a person begins to attack you is to attack them right back, but that's not who I am. I am chosen to be holy and dearly loved by the Father and so my clothing is mercy, kindness, patience, and love toward those who attack me. When I feel weak, His grace makes me strong!

As this lady continued to share the negative opinion she had of me, I remember saying, "Father, remind me of who I am right now!" He spoke with tenderness to my heart as He reminded me that I am qualified and anointed to preach the Good News about Jesus! I remember just drinking that into my soul, and smiling back at the Father! His love was setting my heart free of any fear of being misjudged or my reputation being slandered. All I did was allow Jesus to reestablish my heart in my true identity, and love flowed effortlessly from my heart toward this lady. When she finished talking, I simply replied, "Ma'am, I am so sorry that you feel this way, but the Lord has called me to teach God's people who they are in Christ and the promises they have in Him. And I will continue to tell people of His great love and grace toward them through Jesus. I am sorry that you disagree." My response back to that lady was very peaceful.

> The Apostle Paul admonished us in Romans 13:9 to love from the center of who we are! It's only when we believe the truth that we are dearly loved and forgiven in Jesus, that we have the power to truly love and forgive others.

I remember getting off the phone and being in awe of the work the Spirit of Grace did in my heart. I was clothed in mercy, kindness, and love simply by focusing on Jesus and who I am in Him. I was empowered to love from the center of who I am in Christ. Instead of anger and judgment, my heart was filled with compassion toward this woman. I remember praying, "Father, show her how much you love her. Help her to see that you made her righteous and an heir to all your promises because of Jesus!"

My heart was so established in righteousness that day as I remembered His promise to me to cause my righteousness to shine like the noonday sun! (Psalm 37:6) I remember saying, "Father, You are my vindicator! If You are for me, who can be against me? I am at peace and secure in Your love!"

That's what it looks like to clothe yourself in love! That's what it looks like to love from the center of who you are! When you know and believe that you are chosen, loved, holy and righteous in Jesus, love will be the fruit of your life!

What was the main truth the Holy Spirit taught you from today's study?

_____

_____

_____

_____

_____

_____

_____

_____

Awake to Righteousness

Romans 13:11-14

Pray before you begin.
Ask the Holy Spirit to reveal Jesus to you in the Scriptures.

Today we will study Romans 13:11-14. In these verses the Apostle Paul continues to instruct us in righteous living. He continues to teach us about our new righteous nature in Jesus! He encourages us to wake up and clothe ourselves with the Lord Jesus Christ, and begin living out of our true identity in Him!

> Romans 13:11-14: *[11]This is all the more urgent, for you know how late it is; time is running out. <u>Wake up</u>, for our salvation is nearer now than when we first believed. [12]The night is almost gone; the day of salvation will soon be here. So remove your dark deeds like dirty clothes, and put on the shining armor of light. [13]Because we belong to the day, we must live decent lives for all to see. Don't participate in the darkness of wild parties and drunkenness, or in sexual promiscuity and immoral living, or in quarreling and jealousy. [14]Instead, clothe yourself with the presence of the Lord Jesus Christ. And don't let yourself think about ways to indulge your evil desires.*

Evil deeds are not the fruit of who you are! You are righteous in Jesus! What does the Apostle Paul instruct you to do in verses 11-13?

_____

_____

In verse 14, what does He instruct you to clothe yourself in?

_____

In these verses, the Apostle Paul admonishes us to wake up! Wake up and realize that we have a brand new nature! When we act badly, it is because we either don't know or have forgotten who we truly are in Jesus! James 1:23-24 says, *[23]For if you listen to the word and don't obey, it is like glancing at your face in a mirror. [24]You see yourself, walk away, and forget what you look like.*

Drunkenness, sexual promiscuity, immoral living, quarreling, and jealousy are not who you are! Your Heavenly Father has made you righteous and holy through Jesus! When you clothe yourself with Jesus, you will experience His good, acceptable, and perfect will for every area of your life!

Clothe Yourself with Jesus!

Ephesians 4:23-24: *23Let the Spirit renew your thoughts and attitudes. 24 Put on your new nature, created to be like God — truly righteous and holy.*

What is your new nature? (Ephesians 4:24)

_____

Romans 13:14 instructs you to clothe yourself with Jesus. How do you put on Jesus? How does the fruit of your new nature come out in your life? (Ephesians 4:23)

_____

You clothe yourself with Jesus by letting the spirit of Grace renew your thoughts and attitudes. You are already clothed with righteousness because Jesus gave you His perfect righteousness as a gift. But the amount of righteous fruit you see in your life is a direct result of you receiving God's grace on a daily basis to transform the way you think. When you look to the Spirit of Grace to renew your thoughts and attitudes, you are clothing yourself with Jesus.

First Corinthians 15:34 says, *Awake to righteousness, and do not sin! NKJV* As you awake to the truth that you are truly righteous and holy because of Jesus, sin will no longer have any power in your life. Sin loses its appeal as you begin to enjoy the love, joy, and peace that is found in trusting and relying upon Jesus.

As a young wife, I constantly struggled to be good, because I didn't understand that Jesus had made me a righteous woman as a gift of His grace. I knew Scriptures like Romans 13:13 instructed me not to quarrel, but quite often I found myself in strife with my husband. Because I really wanted to be a godly wife and live in peace, I determined to do better and not argue with my husband the next time around. But it seemed that every time he irritated me, I found myself quarreling with him once again. Relying upon myself only brought a sense of failure and condemnation to my heart and kept me in the vicious cycle of sin.

I can remember when the Spirit of grace began to teach me a better way to live. I called out to Jesus to help me and He began to teach me about the gift of righteousness. My heart was awakened to the truth that I was holy and righteous, not because of what I did, but because of what Jesus had done for me. Just like 1 Corinthians 15:34 says, when I woke up to that truth, sin lost it's power in my life! The power of grace began working in me to resist the temptation to argue, and I began to live in peace instead.

I began to pray, "Father, create in me the desire and the power to do what pleases You (Philippians 2:13). You have made me a righteous and godly wife by your grace. Help me to love, honor, and respect my husband." When I felt tempted to get angry or upset, I would turn my thoughts to Jesus and ask Him to strengthen me by His grace, and I felt His love and peace wash over my mind. I would talk to Him about the way I felt and rely upon Him to renew my mind and attitude. When I began to clothe myself with Jesus, by inviting the Spirit of grace to renew my thoughts and attitude, I began to experience peace in my marriage.

So Awake to Righteousness!

As you allow the Spirit of Grace to renew your thoughts, remember that anger, jealousy, quarreling, and immoral living are not a part of who you are! You have stripped off your old nature, and you now have a brand new nature that is righteous and holy in Christ. Your new nature is one of love, mercy, goodness, kindness, and patience. You are empowered to forgive because you have been forgiven! We all fail at times, but don't let the enemy condemn you! Refocus your mind on Jesus, and let Him reestablish your heart in your righteous identity in Him! When you know and believe that you are righteous in Jesus, righteous fruit will come out in your life, not by your human effort, but by the power of His grace at work in you! Clothe yourself in Jesus! Wake up to your true identity and let the Spirit of Grace renew your thoughts and attitudes so you can experience the glorious life that Jesus purchased for you!

What was the main truth the Holy Spirit taught you from today's study?

_____

_____

_____

_____

_____

_____

_____

No More Judgment; Only Acceptance

Romans 14 and 15:1-7

Day 1

No More Judgment

Day 2

No Condemnation

Day 3

Accept Others as Christ Has Accepted You

No More Judgment

Romans 14:1-12

Pray before you begin.
Ask the Holy Spirit to reveal Jesus to you in the Scriptures.

Today we will take a look at Romans 14:1-12. The Apostle Paul continues instructing us in righteous living. We will see that the fruit of righteousness is a heart of compassion that is free from judging others. When we truly embrace the truth that we have been made righteous not by our good works, but through faith in Jesus, we will begin to see others through our Father's eyes. We will no longer feel the need to argue about our personal convictions, but rather allow the Holy Spirit to lead us each individually. Peace with God and others is the fruit of our lives when we know and believe who we are in Christ.

Romans 14:1-12: *¹Accept other believers who are weak in faith, and don't argue with them about what they think is right or wrong. ²For instance, one person believes it's all right to eat anything. But another believer with a sensitive conscience will eat only vegetables. ³Those who feel free to eat anything must not look down on those who don't. And those who don't eat certain foods must not condemn those who do, <u>for God has accepted them</u>. ⁴Who are you to condemn someone else's servants? Their own master will judge whether they stand or fall. And <u>with the Lord's help, they will stand and receive his approval</u>. ⁵In the same way, some think one day is more holy than another day, while others think every day is alike. You should each be fully convinced that whichever day you choose is acceptable. ⁶Those who worship the Lord on a special day do it to honor Him. Those who eat any kind of food do so to honor the Lord, since they give thanks to God before eating. And those who refuse to eat certain foods also want to please the Lord and give thanks to God. ⁷For we don't live for ourselves or die for ourselves. ⁸<u>If we live, it's to honor the Lord. And if we die, it's to honor the Lord. So whether we live or die, we belong to the Lord</u>. ⁹Christ died and rose again for this very purpose — to be Lord both of the living and of the dead. ¹⁰<u>So why do you condemn another believer? Why do you look down on another believer? Remember, we will all stand before the judgment seat of God</u>. ¹¹For the Scriptures say, "As surely as I live,' says the LORD, 'every knee* *will bend to me, and every tongue will confess allegiance to God.'" ¹²Yes, each of us will give a personal account to God.*

What instructions concerning righteous living does the Apostle Paul give us in Romans 12:1-3?

Verse 1:

_____

Verse 3:

_____

What is the Father's heart toward us all? (verse 3)

_____

With His help, what does our Father want us all to receive? (verse 4)

_____

Our Heavenly Father wants us to follow our heart when it comes to what we eat, drink, or what day we choose to worship Him. What does He want us to be convinced of? (verse 5)

_____

When a believer chooses what they feel is right, what is the motive of their hearts? (verse 6-8)

_____

What is the only judgment that matters? (verses 10-11)

_____

In verse 1, the Apostle Paul instructs us to accept those who are weak in faith, and don't argue with them about what they think is right or wrong. We learned in week 3 that the Greek meaning of the word *faith* is "reliance upon Jesus for salvation." All of us have areas where we are growing in our faith as we learn to rely upon Jesus and not ourselves. Here the Apostle Paul is teaching us to accept others wherever they are in their faith. Arguing doctrine or opinions only separates us, but accepting each other as brothers and sisters in Christ brings unity and love! When we argue, we are really trying to make ourselves right instead of resting in the truth that Jesus made us right. But when our heart is established in the Father's approval and acceptance, we won't feel the need to argue. We will actually be able to disagree with someone's opinion and yet love and accept them anyway. Verse 3 teaches that regardless of a person's personal convictions regarding what is right or wrong, God has accepted them. With His help, we can receive His approval and live at peace with each other. We are approved not because someone agrees with us, but because our Heavenly Father approves of us! Peace with others will be the fruit of our lives when our hearts are established in righteousness.

Whether or not we choose to eat certain foods, or drink certain things, or worship God on a certain day, we all want to honor God in what we do. We honor God when we honor each other by agreeing with what the Father says about us.

In Romans 14:10, the apostle Paul asks the question: *Why do [we] condemn another believer? Why do [we] look down on them? Remember, we will all stand before the judgment seat of God.* It's not my opinion or your opinion that matters. What is most important is that we come into agreement with the Father's judgment and opinion because His opinion is always right!

So how does the Father judge every believer that stands before Him?

> Colossians 1:20-22: *²⁰...and through him God reconciled everything to himself. He made peace with everything in heaven and on earth by means of Christ's blood on the cross. ²¹This includes you who were once far away from God. You were his enemies, separated from him by your evil thoughts and actions. ²²Yet now he has reconciled you to himself through the death of Christ in his physical body. As a result, he has brought you into his own presence, and <u>you are holy and blameless as you stand before him without a single fault</u>.*

When a believer stands before the judgment seat of God, how does the Father judge them?

As believers in Christ, we have been reconciled to the Father. He has made peace with us through the death of Jesus. As a result, He has brought us into His very presence and we stand holy and blameless before Him without a single fault.

> John 3:17-18: *¹⁷For God did not send the Son into the world in order to judge (to reject, to condemn, to pass sentence on) the world, but that the world might find salvation and be made safe and sound through Him. ¹⁸He who believes in Him [who clings to, trusts in, relies on Him] is not judged [he who trusts in Him never comes up for judgment ...].*

What does verse 18 say is true of every person who has placed their faith in Jesus?

_____

Why does this bring peace to your heart?

_____

John 3:17-18 makes it very clear that those who place their faith in Jesus will never be condemned or judged badly by the Father. He sees us in Christ. We are all holy and without fault in His eyes because of Jesus! When we understand this truth and embrace it as our true identity, we will no longer be caught up in judging each other by our personal convictions or actions. Regardless of our differences of opinion in what is right or wrong, we will see each other the way our Father sees us. We will accept each other because He has accepted us!

When your heart is established in righteousness, how will that effect your relationship with others?

_____

_____

What was the main truth the Holy Spirit taught you from today's study?

_____

_____

_____

_____

_____

_____

_____

_____

No More Condemnation

Romans 14:13-23 – 15:1

Pray before you begin.
Ask the Holy Spirit to reveal Jesus to you in the Scriptures.

Today we will study Romans 14:13-23 and Romans 15:1. Remember, grace is the power to live a righteous life. As we grow in our identity in Jesus, our hearts will be transformed and we will love others as Jesus has loved us! Jesus does not condemn or judge us badly. He only reminds us of the truth that we are righteous, holy, approved and accepted in Him! When our own hearts feel condemned, then we will condemn others, but when our hearts are established in righteousness, we are empowered by His grace to see others that same way Jesus sees us!

Romans 14:13-23 through 15:1: *¹³So let's stop condemning each other. Decide instead to live in such a way that you will not cause another believer to stumble and fall. ¹⁴I know and am convinced on the authority of the Lord Jesus that no food, in and of itself, is wrong to eat. But if someone believes it is wrong, then for that person it is wrong. ¹⁵And if another believer is distressed by what you eat, you are not acting in love if you eat it. Don't let your eating ruin someone for whom Christ died. ¹⁶Then you will not be criticized for doing something you believe is good. NLT*

¹⁷[After all] the kingdom of God is not a matter of [getting the] food and drink [one likes], but instead it is righteousness (that state which makes a person acceptable to God) and [heart] peace and joy in the Holy Spirit. ¹⁸He who serves Christ in this way is acceptable and pleasing to God and is approved by men. AMP

¹⁹So let's agree to use all our energy in getting along with each other. Help others with encouraging words; ²⁰don't drag them down by finding fault. MSG

²¹It is better not to eat meat or drink wine or do anything else if it might cause another believer to stumble. ²²You may believe there's nothing wrong with what you are doing, but keep it between yourself and God. Blessed are those who don't feel guilty for doing something they have decided is right. ²³But if you have doubts about whether or not you should eat something, you are sinning if you go ahead and do it. For you are not following your convictions. If you do anything you believe is not right, you are sinning.

Romans 15:1: *We who are strong must be considerate of those who are sensitive about things like this. We must not just please ourselves.*

As righteous children of God, what does verse 13 instruct us to do?

_____

What was the Apostle Paul convinced of? (verse 14)

_____

How can we be considerate of each other? (verses 15-16; 21-23; Romans 15:1)

_____

_____

What is the kingdom of God? (verse 17)

_____

How does a person condemn someone and drag them down? (verse 20)

_____

When grace is at work in our hearts, how will we help others? (verse 19)

_____

_____

The word, *condemn* in Romans 14:13 comes from the Greek word, *krinō* (Strong's G2919) and it means, "to judge: to pronounce an opinion concerning right or wrong; of those who act the part of judges ... in matters of common life, or pass judgment on the words or deeds of others."

In Romans 14:13, the Apostle Paul instructs us to stop condemning each other. Romans 14:10 says, *¹⁰So why do you condemn another believer? Why do you look down on another believer? Remember, we will all stand before the judgment seat of God."* We learned yesterday, that God's judgment of every believer is that in Christ they are holy and without fault in His eyes. He is the final authority and the only one with the power to judge a person. In John 8:1-11 we read the story of Jesus and the adulterous woman. When the teachers of the law wanted to judge her as bad and stone her, Jesus said, *"Let the one who has never sinned throw the first stone!"* The One who has never sinned is the only one who has the authority to judge a person. Since all of the teachers of the Law knew they, too, were guilty of sin, they dropped their stones and walked away. Jesus was the only one who had never sinned, so He was the only one who has the power to judge! As the adulteress stood before Jesus, He declared His judgment of her, saying, *"I do not condemn you!"NASB* He did not judge nor condemn her based on her behavior, instead He wanted to win her heart and transform her life with His great love!

We are just like Jesus! As He is so are we in this world (1 John 4:17) He showed us how a righteous man or woman encourages the heart of a person who has fallen into sin. When you fail, Jesus says the same thing to you, *"I do not condemn you." NASB* When you receive the freedom from condemnation that Jesus offers you, it gives you the power to offer that same gift to others who have failed.

In Romans 14:13-14; 21-23 and Romans 15:1 we have seen that as righteous children of God, we are considerate of one another and how our actions affect each other. We stay true to our personal convictions, without imposing them on others. Each one of us has an individual, personal relationship with Jesus and we are all led by His Spirit. He leads us all differently. What he leads you to do, may not be what He leads someone else to do. What may be right for someone else, may not be right for you! When we understand that we have been made "right" in Jesus, we are free to follow our own hearts, and let others be free to follow theirs!

We all have our opinions of what we think is right or wrong, or what we think is best when it comes to eating, drinking, going to church, or any other personal conviction. I love how the Message Bible translates Romans 14:22: *"Cultivate your own relationship with God, but don't impose it on others."*

Romans 14:17 tells us that the kingdom of God is not a matter of what we think is right or wrong to eat; it's not about trying to follow a set of rules, *but instead it is righteousness (that state which makes a person acceptable to God) and [heart] peace and joy in the Holy Spirit. AMP* In Luke 17:21, Jesus said, *The kingdom of God is within you. NKJV*

Since the kingdom of God is within people's hearts, seeking first the kingdom of God is about building up people! When we share the Good News that righteousness is a gift of God's grace and it produces peace and joy in a person's heart, we are seeking first the kingdom of God! Romans 14:19-20 shows us that living in the kingdom of God is not pointing out people's faults, and trying to get them to live right, but rather it's using all our energy to help others by encouraging them with the truth of who they are in Christ!

Let me share an example from my own life. When I used to believe that the kingdom of God was about doing the right thing, I had all kinds of opinions and judgments about what I thought was right and wrong. I had my opinion about drinking, eating, and going to church, and I looked down on people that didn't believe like me. I was caught in the slavery of the law, and it produced a judgmental heart toward people.

When the Holy Spirit revealed to me that being made righteous was a gift of God's grace, my heart began to change. Instead of looking at people's faults and imposing my personal convictions on them, I began to see people as righteous, valuable, and good because of Jesus! As God's grace did a work in my heart, I let go of my personal opinion and judgments and began to build people up by telling them about their new identity in Christ. No longer judging people by their actions, I was empowered by God's grace to love and accept them right where they were at. I remember when this change took place in my relationship with my husband. Instead of pointing out his faults and telling him what I thought he should do, I began encouraging him with the truth of his identity in Christ. I began to tell him, "You hear from God! You are righteous because of Jesus! You are a success! You have God's favor and everything you put your hand to prospers!" When I began to encourage him with the Father's good opinion of him in Christ, I was seeking first the kingdom of God and I didn't even realize it at the time. The kingdom of God was within my husband! He is righteous, qualified, and blessed because of Jesus! Reminding him of that truth brought peace and joy to both our hearts! And we began to see the blessing of God upon our lives!

In Romans 14:13-23 and Romans 15:1, the Apostle Paul encourages us to no longer condemn people by pointing out their faults, but rather help them through words of encouragement — reminding them of their new identity in Jesus! For the kingdom of God is not about trying to get others to follow a set of rules, but instead it is being made righteous in Jesus and the fruit of joy and peace coming out in our lives by the power of God's Spirit! When we receive God's grace and embrace the truth that we are righteous because of Jesus, we are empowered to share this Good News with others! We live free from condemning and judging others by their actions and begin to see them as righteous, good, valuable, and blessed because of Jesus! There is no more condemnation, only freedom in Christ!

What was the main truth the Holy Spirit taught you from today's study?

_____

_____

_____

_____

Accept Others as Christ Has Accepted You

Romans 15:2-7

Pray before you begin.
Ask the Holy Spirit to reveal Jesus to you in the Scriptures.

In Romans 15:2-7 the Apostle Paul finishes his teaching on living in peace with each other by accepting and loving one another. It is only by God's grace that we can live in harmony with each other and live a life that glorifies God. Grace is the power to live a righteous life!

> Romans 15:2-7: *²We should help others do what is right and build them up in the Lord. ³For even Christ didn't live to please himself. As the Scriptures say, "The insults of those who insult you, O God, have fallen on me." ⁴ Such things were written in the Scriptures long ago to teach us. And the Scriptures give us hope and encouragement as we wait patiently for God's promises to be fulfilled. ⁵May God, who gives this patience and encouragement, help you live in complete harmony with each other, as is fitting for followers of Christ Jesus. ⁶Then all of you can join together with one voice, giving praise and glory to God, the Father of our Lord Jesus Christ. ⁷Therefore, accept each other just as Christ has accepted you so that God will be given glory.*

How can we help someone do what is right? (verse 2)

_____

What do the Scriptures do for each of us? (verse 4)

_____

By His grace, what will God help us do? (verse 5)

_____

How is God given glory through our lives?

Verse 6:

_____

Verse 7:

_____

Why can we fully embrace and accept each other? (verse 7)

_____

In Romans 15:2 the Apostle Paul teaches us once again that we help each other by building one another up in the Lord. Ephesians 4:29 says, *Let no corrupt word proceed out of your mouth, but what is good for necessary edification, that it may impart grace to the hearers. NKJV*

As righteous children of God, our words are an encouragement because we impart grace to those we talk to by building them up in their identity in Christ!

When you hear someone say to you, "You are wonderful! You are patient, kind, and good! You are favored, blessed and accepted by God because of Jesus", what does that do to your heart?

As Romans 15:4 says, the Scriptures give people hope and encouragement as they wait to see the promises of God come to pass in their lives. With God's help, we can live in harmony with each other! We all have our personal opinions about different things in life, and we might not always agree, but we can still live in harmony when we take on the Father's good opinion of each other. Regardless of our personal convictions about certain things, the Father still sees each of us as righteous, good, valuable, and acceptable in His sight.

We learned previously that the glory of God is the Father's good opinion of Himself, and His good opinion of you in Christ! Romans 15:5-6 says that with God's help, we can live in harmony with each other by joining together with one voice and giving glory to God! We do this by only saying what we hear our Father say about each other. When we only say what we hear our Father say, we live in harmony and complete agreement with each other! When we no longer have to convince each other that our opinion is correct, we simply agree that the Father's good opinion is correct and it brings us into agreement.

So what is the Father's good opinion of us all in Christ?

- You are wonderful, and so am I!
- You are good, and so am I!
- You are righteous and so am I!
- You are qualified and so am I!
- You are favored and so am I!
- You are blessed and so am I!
- You are led by God's Spirit and so am I!
- You are patient, loving, and kind, and so am I <u>because of Jesus</u>!

Why is this true about all of us? Because it's our Father's good opinion of us in Christ and He does not lie! (Hebrews 6:17-18)

Our heart attitude and opinion of others is the main indication of whether or not we are living in God's grace and believing that He made us righteous and good. If you are struggling with a judgmental or negative opinion of someone, simply turn to Jesus for His help. Come boldly to His throne of grace, to receive mercy and grace to help you in your time of need (Hebrews 4:15-16). Let His grace transform the way you think about yourself and others!

Rejecting someone or looking down on them because they don't agree with your opinion or because they are doing something you don't agree with is not the fruit of righteousness. When my own heart is tempted to have a negative attitude or opinion of someone, I know it's because I'm not fully trusting what Jesus says about me. At these times, I go to the throne of grace to ask for help in my time of need, and Jesus reminds me that I'm just like Him! I am loved, righteous, kind and good in Christ! With His help, I remember that I am accepted in Him, and His grace empowers me to accept and love others as well!

Romans 5:17 says that when we embrace the gift of righteousness and His overflowing grace, we will live in triumph over sin! We will live free from judging and condemning one another. Instead we will build each other up in the Lord by speaking in agreement with the Father's good opinion of us in Christ. We will live in harmony with each other and with one voice we will glorify our Father in heaven! We accept each other because Jesus has accepted us!

So Awake to Righteousness!

It is not our external rules, nor our opinions regarding what is right or wrong to eat or drink, or observing certain days of worship, that makes us acceptable to God.

Rather, it is our faith in Christ. Be free to be led by God's Spirit in what you do, and give others that freedom too. It is only by God's grace that we can live in harmony with one another and see each other as equal in Christ. As we embrace the gift of righteousness, and God's overflowing grace, there will be no more judging each other, but only acceptance as we see each other in the same way that the Father sees us. We will be of one heart and mind, agreeing with our Father's good opinion of each other, and truly living a life that glorifies Him!

What was the main truth the Holy Spirit taught you from today's study?

_____
_____
_____
_____
_____
_____
_____

As you read today's lesson, did anyone come to mind that you have been struggling with negative thoughts or attitudes toward?

_____
_____
_____
_____
_____

Take time right now to go to the throne of grace and talk to Jesus. Ask Him to help you see yourself and that person through His eyes. Let His grace transform your heart and life!

DAY 3

The Righteous Glorify God

Romans 15:8-33 and 16

Day 1

The Righteous Glorify God

Day 2

The Righteous Place Their Hope in Jesus

Day 3

Paul's Mission, Greetings, and Warnings

The Righteous Glorify God

Romans 15:8-11

Pray before you begin.
Ask the Holy Spirit to reveal Jesus to you in the Scriptures.

This week we will finish our study on the Book of Romans. Today we will read Romans 15:8-11 and continue to see a picture of the fruit of our lives when we truly awake to righteousness and embrace our new identity in Jesus! When you live out of the truth that you have been made the righteousness of God in Christ Jesus, your life will glorify God.

> Romans 15:8-11: *⁸Remember that Christ came as a servant to the Jews to show that God is true to the promises he made to their ancestors. ⁹He also came so that the Gentiles might give glory to God for his mercies to them. That is what the psalmist meant when he wrote: "For this, I will praise you among the Gentiles; I will sing praises to your name." ¹⁰And in another place it is written, "Rejoice with his people, you Gentiles." ¹¹And yet again, "Praise the LORD, all you Gentiles. Praise him, all you people of the earth."*

Why did Jesus come as a servant to the Jews? (verse 8)

_____

Why did He come to the Gentiles? (verse 9)

_____

What flows from our hearts when we understand God's mercy toward us? (verses 9-11)

_____

_____

Jesus came to the Jews to show that God is true to His promises to them. God promised Abraham that through him all the people of the earth would be blessed! We learned in Galatians 3:1-14 that the blessing promised to Abraham was the gift of righteousness through faith in Jesus! Jesus came to the Gentiles to tell them the Good News that they were included in this promise. We would be declared righteous: innocent, blameless, justified, and qualified for all of God's favor and blessing, not through any work of our own, but through the finished work of Jesus! Romans 15:9 says that when we receive His mercy toward us, we will glorify God! When we truly understand His great love and mercy toward us, our hearts are filled with thanksgiving and praise for all He has done for us! The word *glory* in verse 9 comes from the word *glorify* and it means "to praise, to celebrate, to honor, to cause the dignity and worth of a person to become manifested and acknowledged." (Strong's G1391, BLB)

Praise and thanksgiving used to be just another work I needed to do to please God. I would hear sermons on the importance of praising and thanking God and I would add it to my "to do" list to qualify myself. I remember many times going to church and not feeling worthy to praise God because I had just been in strife with my husband and I felt like a failure. Have you ever had one of those day when you were on your way to church and you got frustrated, angry or impatient with someone in your family and by the time you got there you didn't feel like praising God? The reason we felt this way is because our attention is on our failure rather than our Father's mercy toward us! A person does not need mercy unless they have failed in some way. When we realize that no matter how we have failed, our Father's view and opinion of us never changes, genuine praise and glory toward Him flows from our hearts!

We Glorify Our Father Because He First Glorified Us!

Romans 8: 29-30: "*²⁹For those whom He foreknew [of whom He was aware and loved beforehand], He also destined from the beginning [foreordaining them] to be molded into the image of His Son [and share inwardly His likeness], that He might become the firstborn among many brethren. ³⁰And those whom He thus foreordained, He also called; and those whom He called, He also justified (acquitted, made righteous, putting them into right standing with Himself). And those whom He justified, He also glorified [raising them to a heavenly dignity and condition or state of being]." AMP*

What did your Heavenly Father do for you so that you would be molded into the very image of Jesus and share inwardly His nature and likeness? How did He show His mercy toward you? (verse 30)

The word *glorified* in Romans 8:30 has the exact same meaning as the word *glorify* in Romans 15:9. Your Heavenly Father called you to be His own, made you righteousness, and has glorified you through Jesus! He praises and honors you as His beloved child and He caused your dignity and worth to be manifested and acknowledged by the great price Jesus paid to make you His own!

When we focus on the Good News of our Heavenly Father's mercy and grace toward us in Jesus, praise and thanksgiving springs forth from our hearts! No one needs to teach us how we need to praise and thank God more. It's the Good News of His gift of righteousness that causes our hearts to glorify Him! We glorify Him because He first glorified us! We love Him because He first loved us!

> 2 Corinthians 4:15: *All of this is for your benefit. And as God's grace reaches more and more people, there will be great thanksgiving, and God will receive more and more glory.*

As more and more people hear the Good News of God's grace, what will be the result?

_____

The word *glory* in this verse means "always a good opinion concerning one, resulting in praise, honor and glory!" (Strong's G1380, BLB) As the true Good News of our Heavenly Father's love and grace reaches more people, there will be great thanksgiving in the hearts of men as they see Him for who He truly is — a good, loving, merciful Father who adores and glorifies His children! Many believers have a bad opinion of God because they don't really know Him. They accuse God of bringing trials and sickness, and judging people for their sin. Those are very bad opinions of God and they do not glorify Him at all! They do not reveal His true character and love for His children and the world. When we glorify our Father, we have a good opinion of Him! When we say things like, "Father, You are wonderful and good! Your mercy endures forever! Every good and perfect gift comes from you! I love You because You first loved me! That's how you glorify your Father in heaven, by having a good opinion of Him, because He has a good opinion of you.

> When we remember how Jesus has clothed us in salvation and covered us with a robe of righteousness and made us His beautiful, beloved bride, our hearts are overwhelmed with His unconditional, unchanging love for us!

> Isaiah 61:10 says: *[10]I will greatly rejoice in the Lord, my soul will exult in my God; for He has clothed me with the garments of salvation, He has covered me with the robe of righteousness, as a bridegroom decks himself with a garland, and as a bride adorns herself with her jewels. AMP*

When we remember how Jesus has clothed us in salvation and covered us with a robe of righteousness and made us His beautiful, beloved bride, our hearts are overwhelmed with His unconditional, unchanging love for us! He qualified us and made us joint heirs with Him! Everything He has and is belongs to us! We have something to rejoice about!

He glorified you by giving you His perfect righteousness. When you truly embrace His gift of righteousness to you, praising and glorifying Him is no longer an effort or something you need to add to your "to do" list, it simply flows from your heart because you realize just how much you are loved! You glorify Him because He first glorified you!

What was the main truth the Holy Spirit taught you from today's study?

_____

_____

_____

_____

_____

_____

_____

_____

The Righteous Place Their Hope in Jesus

Romans 15:12-19

Pray before you begin.
Ask the Holy Spirit to reveal Jesus to you in the Scriptures.

In Romans 15:12-19 the Apostle Paul once again reminds us of who we are in Jesus. We see the power of grace that is at work in our lives when we embrace the gift of righteousness by placing our hope in Jesus!

Romans 15:12-19: *12And in another place Isaiah said, "The heir to David's throne will come, and he will rule over the Gentiles. They will place their hope on him." 13I pray that God, the source of hope, will fill you completely with joy and peace because you trust in him. Then you will overflow with confident hope through the power of the Holy Spirit. 14I am fully convinced, my dear brothers and sisters, that you are full of goodness. You know these things so well you can teach each other all about them. 15Even so, I have been bold enough to write about some of these points, knowing that all you need is this reminder....16I am a special messenger from Christ Jesus to you Gentiles. I bring you the Good News so that I might present you as an acceptable offering to God, made holy by the Holy Spirit. 17So I have reason to be enthusiastic about all Christ Jesus has done through me in my service to God. 18Yet I dare not boast about anything except what Christ has done through me, bringing the Gentiles to God by my message and by the way I worked among them. 19They were convinced by the power of miraculous signs and wonders and by the power of God's Spirit. In this way, I have fully presented the Good News of Christ from Jerusalem all the way to Illyricum.*

Where do the righteous children of God place their hope? (verse 12)

_____

What does the Spirit of Grace do in our hearts when we trust and rely upon Jesus? (verse 13)

_____

114

How did the Apostle Paul encourage us in our new identity in verse 14? What did he say was true about you?

_____

What can you do now that you know this truth so well? (verse 14)

_____

What was the Good News that the Apostle Paul brought to us? (verse 16)

_____

In verses 18 and 19 we see that the Apostle Paul knew where his strength and power came from. Did he depend on himself or Jesus?

_____

When we awake to righteousness, our hope is in Jesus alone. We no longer put our hope in our own effort, our own plans, or our own good works. Our hope is in Him as our righteousness. We come to realize that our identity is not based on our circumstances or our good or bad behavior, but rather on the finished work of Jesus! I personally, have placed my hope in a certain outcome or my own ability. There have been times in my life when I prayed about certain situations, but the truth was my hope was in a job, a person, or a way that I wanted things to work out well for me, but I often ended up disappointed. Romans 9:33 says that those who place their hope in Jesus will never be disappointed!

I have come to realize that if I want to live free from disappointment, I must put my hope in Jesus, alone, as my righteousness! In other words, when I look to Him as my provision, my healer, my wisdom, my approval, and my strength, He never fails to encourage my heart and empower me to believe! When I give the "how" and the "when" over into his hands, He works all things together for my good just like He promised. He is the one who qualified us for all of God's promises! Just like the Apostle Paul prayed in Romans 15:13, Jesus is the source of our hope, and He fills our hearts with joy and peace as we trust Him! When we feel weak, He empowers us to believe as we look to Him for strength. In our weakness, He makes us strong! (2 Corinthians 12:9)

Jesus gave us a perfect example of what it looks like to fully put our trust in the Father. In the Garden of Gethsemane, when Jesus was getting ready to lay His life down for us, He had a moment of weakness. The Scripture tells us that His heart was filled with fear and He sweat great drops of blood. But in His moment of weakness, He put His hope in the Father's great love for Him! He looked to the Father for strength and He was empowered by the Holy Spirit to finish the work the Father sent Him to do. He surrendered His opinion and will to the Father's and placed His whole life in His Father's hands! When you trust Jesus you are exchanging your ability and your opinion for His. Just like Jesus, sometimes our hearts are filled with fear concerning a situation in our lives, but if we look to the Father for everything we need, He will fill our hearts with joy and peace, and we will be empowered with confident hope by the power of His Spirit!

The Righteous Encourage Others to Place Their Hope in Jesus

In Romans 15:14-16, the Apostle Paul once again reminds us of our true identity in Jesus. He says, "I am fully convinced, dear brothers and sisters, that you are full of goodness! I have brought you the Good News that you have been made holy in Christ!" You are full of goodness and have been made holy because you are one with Jesus! He is good, and He made you good! He is holy and He made you holy! That is the Good News of the Gospel! Throughout the Book of Romans, the Apostle Paul reminds us over and over again that we have been made righteous, not through our good works, but through faith in Jesus! Saying You are "good and holy" is just another way of saying, "You are righteous!" He goes on to say you know this so well, you can now tell others, that they, too, are good because of Jesus! When you place your hope in Jesus, you are used by Him to encourage others to put their hope in Him as well.

As your heart becomes established in righteousness and the love of the Father, sharing this Good News will come as easy as breathing. It is who you are — a minister of God's grace.

> Second Corinthians 5:18-21: *¹⁸But all things are from God, Who through Jesus Christ reconciled us to Himself [received us into favor, brought us into harmony with Himself] and gave to us the ministry of reconciliation [that by word and deed we might aim to bring others into harmony with Him]. ¹⁹It was God [personally present] in Christ, reconciling and restoring the world to favor with Himself, not counting up and holding against [men] their trespasses [but cancelling them], and committing to us the message of reconciliation (of the restoration to favor). ²⁰So we are Christ's ambassadors, God making His appeal as it were through us. We [as Christ's personal representatives] beg you for His sake to lay hold of the divine favor [now offered you] and be reconciled to God. ²¹For our sake He made Christ [virtually] to be sin Who knew no sin, so that in and through Him we might become [endued with, viewed as being in, and examples of] the righteousness of God [what we ought to be, approved and acceptable and in right relationship with Him, by His goodness].*

What did your Heavenly Father do for you through Jesus? (verse 18)

_____

_____

Your Heavenly Father called you to the ministry of reconciliation. According to the Amplified Bible what is the ministry of reconciliation? (verse 18)

_____

As Christ's ambassador and a minister of reconciliation, what Good News does the Father want you to share with people? (verses 19 and 21)

_____

_____

In Romans 15:18 the Apostle Paul revealed that his hope and confidence was not in anything he said or did, but it was in Jesus who was working in him! He did not boast about the great works he did, but rather the great work that Jesus did in and through him as he shared the Good News with others! Just like the Apostle Paul, we have all been called to the ministry of reconciliation — bringing others into harmony with the Father by telling them He is not holding any of their sins against them. We do not boast in anything we have done, but rather what Jesus has done in us! Jesus lives in us, lives through us, and speaks through us. We are His hands, His feet, and His mouth in this world. The scripture says, "How beautiful are the feet of them who bring Good News!" (Isaiah 52:7). You are Christ's ambassador! You have heard the Good News that righteousness is a free gift of God's grace and you are good and holy because of Jesus! Now you can boldly and confidently share this Good News with others by encouraging them to place their hope in Jesus as well.

What was the main truth the Holy Spirit taught you from today's study?

_____

_____

_____

_____

_____

_____

Paul's Mission, Greetings and Warnings

Romans 15:20-33 and 16

Pray before you begin.
Ask the Holy Spirit to reveal Jesus to you in the Scriptures.

Today is the final day of our study of the Book of Romans. As we read chapters 15:20-33 through chapter 16, Paul explains his mission in sharing the Good News and greets his fellow ministers in Christ. He ends by warning us to guard our hearts from any other message that contradicts the true Good News: That righteousness is a gift of God's grace through Jesus!

Paul's Mission to Share the Good News

Romans 15:20-33: *²⁰My ambition has always been to preach the Good News where the name of Christ has never been heard, rather than where a church has already been started by someone else. ²¹I have been following the plan spoken of in the Scriptures, where it says, "Those who have never been told about him will see, and those who have never heard of him will understand." ²²In fact, my visit to you has been delayed so long because I have been preaching in these places. ²³But now I have finished my work in these regions, and after all these long years of waiting, I am eager to visit you. ²⁴I am planning to go to Spain, and when I do, I will stop off in Rome. And after I have enjoyed your fellowship for a little while, you can provide for my journey. ²⁵But before I come, I must go to Jerusalem to take a gift to the believers there. ²⁶For you see, the believers in Macedonia and Achaia have eagerly taken up an offering for the poor among the believers in Jerusalem. ²⁷They were glad to do this because they feel they owe a real debt to them. Since the Gentiles received the spiritual blessings of the Good News from the believers in Jerusalem, they feel the least they can do in return is to help them financially. ²⁸As soon as I have delivered this money and completed this good deed of theirs, I will come to see you on my way to Spain. ²⁹And I am sure that when I come, Christ will richly bless our time together. ³⁰Dear brothers and sisters, I urge you in the name of our Lord*

Jesus Christ to join in my struggle by praying to God for me. Do this because of your love for me, given to you by the Holy Spirit. ³¹Pray that I will be rescued from those in Judea who refuse to obey God. Pray also that the believers there will be willing to accept the donation I am taking to Jerusalem. ³²Then, by the will of God, I will be able to come to you with a joyful heart, and we will be an encouragement to each other. ³³And now may God, who gives us His peace, be with you all. Amen.

Paul's Greetings

Romans 16:1-16: *¹I commend to you our sister Phoebe, who is a deacon in the church in Cenchrea. ²Welcome her in the Lord as one who is worthy of honor among God's people. Help her in whatever she needs, for she has been helpful to many, and especially to me. ³Give my greetings to Priscilla and Aquila, my co-workers in the ministry of Christ Jesus. ⁴In fact, they once risked their lives for me. I am thankful to them, and so are all the Gentile churches. ⁵Also give my greetings to the church that meets in their home. Greet my dear friend Epenetus. He was the first person from the province of Asia to become a follower of Christ. ⁶Give my greetings to Mary, who has worked so hard for your benefit. ⁷Greet Andronicus and Junia, my fellow Jews, who were in prison with me. They are highly respected among the apostles and became followers of Christ before I did. ⁸Greet Ampliatus, my dear friend in the Lord. ⁹Greet Urbanus, our co-worker in Christ, and my dear friend Stachys. ¹⁰Greet Apelles, a good man whom Christ approves. And give my greetings to the believers from the household of Aristobulus. ¹¹Greet Herodion, my fellow Jew. Greet the Lord's people from the household of Narcissus. ¹²Give my greetings to Tryphena and Tryphosa, the Lord's workers, and to dear Persis, who has worked so hard for the Lord. ¹³Greet Rufus, whom the Lord picked out to be His very own; and also his dear mother, who has been a mother to me. ¹⁴Give my greetings to Asyncritus, Phlegon, Hermes, Patrobas, Hermas, and the brothers and sisters who meet with them. ¹⁵Give my greetings to Philologus, Julia, Nereus and his sister, and to Olympas and all the believers who meet with them. ¹⁶Greet each other in Christian love. All the churches of Christ send you their greetings.*

Paul's Warnings about False Teaching

Romans 16:17-27: *¹⁷And now I make one more appeal, my dear brothers and sisters. Watch out for people who cause divisions and upset people's faith by* *teaching things contrary to what you have been taught. Stay away from them. ¹⁸Such people are not serving Christ our Lord; they are serving their own personal interests. By smooth talk and glowing words they deceive innocent people. ¹⁹But everyone knows that you are obedient to the Lord. This makes me very happy. I want you to be wise in doing right and to stay innocent of any wrong. ²⁰The God of peace will soon crush Satan under your feet. May the grace of our Lord Jesus be with you. ²¹Timothy, my fellow worker, sends you his greetings, as do Lucius, Jason, and Sosipater, my fellow Jews.*

²²I, Tertius, the one writing this letter for Paul, send my greetings, too, as one of the Lord's followers. ²³Gaius says hello to you. He is my host and also serves as host to the whole church. Erastus, the city treasurer, sends you his greetings, and so does our brother Quartus. ²⁴May the grace of our Lord Jesus Christ be with you all. Amen.

²⁵Now all glory to God, who is able to make you strong, just as my Good News says. This message about Jesus Christ has revealed his plan for you Gentiles, a plan kept secret from the beginning of time. ²⁶But now as the prophets foretold and as the eternal God has commanded, this message is made known to all Gentiles everywhere, so that they too might believe and obey him. ²⁷All glory to the only wise God, through Jesus Christ, forever. Amen.

What was the Apostle Paul's last appeal in the Book of Romans? (Romans 16:17)

_____

_____

What did He say about people whose teachings contradict the true Gospel of Grace? (Romans 16:18)

_____

_____

What does the Good News say? (Romans 16:25)

_____

Why was the Good News made known to the Gentiles? (Romans 16:26)

_____

In Romans 16:17-20, the Apostle Paul warns us to stay away from teaching that is contrary to what he taught in the Book of Romans. He tells us that those who teach that we are qualified for God's approval and blessing by our good works and our obedience to the law are serving their own personal interests. By their charismatic words and smooth talk they are deceiving people who are already innocent, blameless, and qualified because of Jesus!

Throughout the Book of Romans, the Apostle Paul reminded us of the Good News over and over again. He taught us that:

- Righteousness is a free gift of God's grace. You can't earn it by your good works. It is received through faith in Jesus!

- There is no condemnation to those who are in Christ Jesus!

- Jesus died to forgive all our sins and absolve us of all guilt before God!

- He rose again to secure our righteousness forever!

- Those who receive God's gift of righteousness and overflowing grace will triumph over sin!

- Grace is the power to live a righteous life and glorify God!

- We are one with Jesus and heirs of His glory and nothing can separate us from His love!

Since you have heard the true Gospel in the Book of Romans, you are now equipped to recognize any message that does not point to Jesus and His finished work. If the message points to you and what you need to do, it's not the Gospel! If the message points to Jesus and what He did for you, it's the Good News! When we live in God's grace we will live productive lives, and produce righteous fruit because that's who we are in Jesus! For as He is so are we in this world!

The Apostle Paul said in Romans 16:26 that the Good News was preached to the Gentiles so that they might believe and obey. True obedience in the New Covenant is trusting and relying upon Jesus (John 6:28-29; 1 John 4:22-24). When you believe who you are in Jesus, righteousness will be the fruit of your life!

So Awake to Righteousness!

You were created to be loved and to glorify your Father in heaven! It is He who makes you strong and establishes you in your new identity in Jesus. So let go of your own effort and good works and completely rely upon Jesus as your righteousness, and watch as the manifestation of who He is in you springs forth in every area of your life! The power of God's grace is at work in our lives when we embrace the gift of righteousness!

Heavenly Father, Thank You for the gift of righteousness You have given me through Jesus! Today I embrace my true identity in Christ! I am forgiven! I am loved! I am accepted and approved! I am righteous! I am free from sin! I am innocent! I am qualified! I am empowered to live a righteous life because of Jesus! I will no longer listen to the lies that tell me that I have to qualify myself for Your blessings upon my life, for Jesus has already qualified me! I will no longer live in the shame or condemnation of my sin! Jesus paid too great a price to set me free! Your grace is all I need to live a righteous life that truly glorifies You! Help me to not rely upon myself, but to rely completely on You! I love You, Father, because I know You love me and nothing can ever separate me from Your great love!

What was the main truth the Holy Spirit taught you from today's study?

_____

_____

_____

_____

_____

_____

_____

_____

Holy Bible Special Hebrew–Greek Key Study Edition copyright © 1984 by Spiros Zodhiates and AMG International, Inc.

Merriam Webster's College Dictionary, 10th Edition copyright © 1994 by Merriam-Webster, Inc.

Strong's Exhaustive Concordance of the Bible

Thorndike Barnhart Intermediate Dictionary

Vine's Expository Dictionary of New Testament Words

Marvin Vincent Word Studies in the New Testament

Blue Letter Bible (BLB) www.blueletterbible.org

We would love to hear how this Bible Study has impacted your life.

To contact the author, write:

Connie Witter
Because of Jesus Ministries
P.O. Box 3064
Broken Arrow, OK 74013-3064

Or email:

Connie@becauseofJesus.com

For additional copies of this book go to:

www.becauseofJesus.com
Or call 918-994-6500

Connie Witter is a speaker, author, and Bible Study teacher. Her best-selling book, *P.S. God Loves You*, has sold over 150,000 copies. She is the founder of Because of Jesus Ministries, which was established in 2006 and has been teaching Bible Studies for over twenty years. Her first Bible Study, Because of Jesus, was published in 2002 and is the foundation for her life and ministry. Since 2005, she has held an annual Because of Jesus Women's Conference, and has also spoken at other women's ministry conferences in Tulsa, and across the United States.

Connie's travels have taken her across the United States as well as Russia, as she shares the life-changing message of *Because of Jesus*. She has been the guest speaker at churches, conferences and retreats, and has also spoken into the lives of teenage girls. She has been a guest on several Christian TV and radio programs, as well as is featured on the Grace United radio station. Her own weekly TV program, *Because of Jesus*, can be seen worldwide through her ministry website, *www.becauseofJesus.com*, as well as on several channels across the United States. Each week Connie shares the Good News that we are righteous, valuable, precious, blessed, favored and extravagantly loved by God, because of Jesus. Thousands of lives across the world have been changed through her ministry.

If you are interested in having Connie speak at your event you can contact her at: connie@becauseofjesus.com.

Other Bible Studies by Connie Witter

Awake to Righteousness Volume 1
Because of Jesus Bible Study
Living Loved Living Free Bible Study

Books by Connie Witter

P.S. God Loves You
21 Days to Discover Who You Are in Jesus
Living Loved Living Free
The Inside Story Teen Devotional
The Inside Story for Girls Devotional
The Chicken Head Story — A Children's Book

CD/DVD Series by Connie Witter

Because of Jesus
Living Loved, Living Free
Awake to Righteousness Volume 1 and 2
It is Finished — A Study on the Book of Hebrews
Forsaking Religion Embracing Relationship: A Study on the Book of Galatians
Christ in You — The Hope of Glory: A Study on the Book of Colossians
God's Abundant Provision of Grace: Experiencing Financial Freedom in Christ
The Lord is My Shepherd — Psalm 23
The Gospel of John
The Greatest Love Story Ever Told — Song of Songs

To order any of these products go to: www.becauseofjesus.com

Made in the USA
Middletown, DE
04 May 2023

30010506R00073